Ancient Ballads
Traditionally Sung in New England

From the Helen Hartness Flanders Ballad Collection
Middlebury College, Middlebury, Vermont

Compiled and Edited by
HELEN HARTNESS FLANDERS

Correlated with the numbered
Francis James Child Collection

VOLUME II • Ballads 53-93

D1197963

V. 2

Critical Analyses by **Tristam P. Coffin**

Music Annotations by **Bruno Nettl**

Philadelphia · University of Pennsylvania Press

Printed in the United States of America

Contents

Transcribers of Tunes

Transcribers are identified by initial:

> M. O.—Marguerite Olney
> H. E. F. B.—Elizabeth Flanders Ballard
> P. B.—Phillips Barry
> G. B.—George Brown
> A. B.—Alice Brown
> H. H. F.—Helen Hartness Flanders

All tunes in Volume II were transcribed by M. O. except as noted below:

Child Number	Version	Transcriber
53	H	G. B.
53	T	H. E. F. B.
54		H. E. F. B.
67		H. E. F. B.
68		P. B.
73	A	G. B.
73	B	H. E. F. B.
73	E	H. E. F. B.
73	F	P. B.
73	I	A. B.
73	K	G. B.
74	A	H. E. F. B.
74	G	H. E. F. B.
74	H	H. E. F. B.
75	C	H. E. F. B.
75	L	Enid Crawford Pierce (Mrs. John)

Child Number	Version	Transcriber
81	B	H. E. F. B.
81	E	H. E. F. B.
81	F	G. B.
81	I	H. E. F. B.
84	D	H. E. F. B.
84	G	G. B.
84	H²	H. H. F.
84	N	H. E. F. B.
84	P	H. E. F. B.
93	D¹	H. E. F. B.
93	D²	H. E. F. B.
93	E	H. E. F. B.
93	F	H. E. F. B.

Abbreviations Used
in the Headnotes to the Ballads

Books

Aarne-Thompson: Aarne, Antti and Thompson, Stith. *Types of the Folk-Tale* (Folklore Fellows Communications 74, Helsinki, 1928).

Barry: Barry, Phillips and others. *British Ballads from Maine* (New Haven, 1929).

Belden: Belden, H. M. *Ballads and Songs Collected by the Missouri Folklore Society* (University of Missouri Studies, XV, Columbia, Mo., 1940).

Boggs: Boggs, Ralph. *Index of Spanish Tales* (Folklore Fellows Communications 90, Helsinki, 1930).

Child: Child, Francis J. *The English and Scottish Popular Ballads* (5 vols.; Boston, 1882-1898).

Coffin: Coffin, Tristram P. *The British Traditional Ballad in North America* (Philadelphia, 1950).

Dean-Smith: Dean-Smith, Margaret. *A Guide to English Folk Song Collections, 1822-1952* (Liverpool, 1954).

Greig and Keith: Greig, Gavin and Keith, Alexander. *Last Leaves of Traditional Ballads, etc.* (Aberdeen, 1925).

Laws, *ABBB:* Laws, G. Malcolm. *American Balladry from British Broadsides* (Philadelphia, 1957).

Ord: Ord, John. *The Bothy Songs and Ballads of Aberdeen, Banff, and Moray, etc.* (Paisley, 1930).

Periodicals

BFSSNE: Bulletin of the Folk-Song Society of the Northeast, I-XII (Cambridge, Mass., 1930-37).

FFC: Folklore Fellows Communications (Helsinki, 1922——).

HFQ: Hoosier Folklore Quarterly (Bloomington, Indiana, 1942-50).

JAF: Journal of American Folklore (Philadelphia, 1888——).

JFSS: Journal of the Folk-Song Society (London, 1899-1936).

MLN: Modern Language Notes (Baltimore, 1886——).

NYFQ: New York Folklore Quarterly (Ithaca, New York, 1945——).

PMLA: Publications of the Modern Language Association (Baltimore, 1886——).

SFQ: Southern Folklore Quarterly (Gainesville, Florida, 1937——).

WF: Western Folklore (Berkeley, California, 1942——).

Other books are given with complete title, date, and place of publication, and other pertinent information when mentioned in the headnotes. References to previous publications by Mrs. Flanders are given by the title of the book.

Ballads Migrant in New England (with M. Olney [New York, 1953]).

Country Songs of Vermont (with H. Norfleet [New York, 1937]).

A Garland of Green Mountain Song (with H. Norfleet [Boston, 1934]).

The New Green Mountain Songster (with E. Ballard, P. Barry, and G. Brown [New Haven, 1939]).

Vermont Folk-Songs & Ballads (with G. Brown [Brattleboro, Vt., 1931]).

Abbreviations Used to Refer to Tune Collections in the Musical Annotations

AA Arnold, Byron, *Folksongs of Alabama* (University, Alabama: University of Alabama Press, 1950).

BC1 Bronson, Bertrand Harris, *The Traditional Tunes of the Child Ballads* (Princeton, N. J.: Princeton University Press, 1959) Vol. I.

BES Barry, Eckstorm, and Smyth, *British Ballads from Maine* (New Haven: Yale University Press, 1929).

BF Barry, Phillips, *Folk Music in America* (New York: National Service Bureau, 1939).

BI Brewster, Paul G., *Ballads and Songs of Indiana* (Bloomington: Indiana University, 1940).

BM Belden, Henry M., *Ballads and Songs Collected by the Missouri Folk-Lore Society* (Columbia: University of Missouri, 1940).

BP Bayard, Samuel P., "The British Folk Tradition" in George Korson (ed.), *Pennsylvania Songs and Legends* (Philadelphia: University of Pennsylvania Press, 1949).

CNS Creighton, Helen, *Songs and Ballads from Nova Scotia* (Toronto: J. M. Dent & Sons, 1932).

CS Cox, John Harrington, *Folk-Songs of the South* (Cambridge: Harvard University Press, 1925).

CWV Cox, John Harrington, *Folk-Songs mainly from West Virginia* (New York: National Service Bureau, 1939).

DV Davis, Arthur Kyle, *Traditional Ballads of Virginia* (Cambridge: Harvard University Press, 1929).

EO Eddy, Mary Olive, *Ballads and Songs from Ohio* (New York: J. J. Augustin, 1939).

FCB4   *The Frank C. Brown Collection of North Carolina Folklore,* Vol. IV, "The Music of the Ballads" (ed.) Jan P. Schinhan (Durham, N. C.; Duke University Press, 1958).

GCM   Gardner, Emelyn E. and Chickering, Geraldine J., *Ballads and Songs of Southern Michigan* (Ann Arbor: University of Michigan Press, 1939).

GN   Greenleaf, Elisabeth B. (ed.), *Ballads and Songs of Newfoundland* (Cambridge: Harvard University Press, 1933).

LNE   Linscott, Eloise H., *Folk Songs of Old New England* (New York: Macmillan, 1939).

MF   Morris, Alton C., *Folksongs of Florida* (Gainesville: University of Florida Press, 1950).

MK   McGill, Josephine, *Folk Songs of the Kentucky Mountains* (New York: Bossey, 1917).

RO1   Randolph, Vance, *Ozark Folksongs,* Vol. I (Columbia; The State Historical Society of Missouri, 1946-1950).

SAA   Smith, Reed, *American Anthology of Old World Ballads* (New York: J. Fisher & Bro., 1937).

Sharp1 Sharp, Cecil James, *English Folk Songs from the Southern Appalachians,* Vol. I (2nd and enlarged edition; London, New York: Oxford University Press, 1952).

SSC   Smith, Reed, *South Carolina Ballads* (Cambridge: Harvard University Press, 1928).

WBT   Wells, Evelyn K., *The Ballad Tree* (New York: Ronald Press Co., 1950).

Child Ballads 13, 14 C, 45 B^3, 53 F, 79 A, 105 A, 140 A^2, and 278 L are to be found on the long-playing record, New England Folksong Series No. 1, issued and distributed by Middlebury College.

Ancient Ballads

Traditionally Sung in New England

Young Beichan

(Child 53)

This ballad has an extensive Anglo-American tradition and still is well known on both sides of the Atlantic. The American songs all trace back to early broadsides and song books and quite generally refer to the hero as Lord Bateman or Bakeman. These texts vary somewhat in minor detail, but follow the Child L pattern as to plot outline, significant facts, and length. Nevertheless, a good many scholars have devoted a good bit of time to the minor variations of the American versions and more particularly to identifying the printed sources of the ballad in the New World. George L. Kittredge (*JAF*, XXX, 295-97) used "the hole bored in the hero's shoulder" as a means of distinguishing texts closely akin to Child L from those related to the Coverly broadside in the Isaiah Thomas Collection, Worcester, Massachusetts, and Phillips Barry, *British Ballads from Maine*, 106 f., continues the probings and points out the "hole in the shoulder" stanza is characteristic of the South. There is also a good bit of information along similar lines in Jane Zielonko's Master's thesis, "Some American Variants of Child Ballads" (Columbia University, 1945), 83 f.

The Flanders versions below have been divided according to the findings of these researchers. Texts A-J seem to be similar to the Coverly broadside or to the version printed in the J. S. Locke of Boston *Forget-Me-Not Songster* (See A particularly) that goes back to an earlier broadside Coverly may have used. K-S are close to the text printed by Lucy

9

E. Broadwood and J. A. F. Maitland in *English Country
Songs* (London, 1893) and cited by Barry, *op. cit.,* 116. This
is a form of the song still known in Britain that evidently
found its way into print in New England. In this series
(see K-O) the hero's shoulder is not bored through as in
many Child texts, but Bateman is tied to a tree. T, it will
be noted, contains further modifications and a compression
of the narrative. But, all in all, the Flanders texts are
pretty typical of the northern findings for this ballad.

Child, I, 455 f., discusses the affinities of this song and the
legend associated with Gilbert à Becket in the Middle Ages.
However, analogous stories are known about Henry of
Brunswick, Alexander von Metz, and a host of other heroes
in Scandinavian and southern European balladry. A start
on a bibliography can be had in Coffin, 63-65 (American);
Dean-Smith, 5 (English) ; Greig and Keith, 40-43 (Scottish) ;
and the notes in Child. Kittredge's *JAF* article contains a
number of references, not easily available elsewhere, to
printed American texts of "Lord Bateman" and its relative
"The Turkish Lady." The latter, listed by Laws as O 26 and
possibly derived from "Lord Bateman," is also immensely
popular in America. Laws, *ABBB,* 238, and Coffin, 65, give a
good many references for it.

The eight tunes for Child 53 are all related, and all
correspond to tune group A in BC1. Two subfamilies appear: 1) the Davis, Kennison, Pierce, and Burke tunes,
characterized by a triad at the beginning; this group corresponds to BC1 group Aa. The other tunes together fit in
with BC1 group Ab, the Morton tune being relatively divergent from the others, however.

A

Jointly remembered by the three daughters of Edward O. Young—Mrs. Florence Underhill and the Misses Young— of Bellows Falls. Mr. Young possessed a Forget-Me-Not- Songster *from which he undoubtedly learned the words, since there are almost no verbal changes when they were set down from memory and as he sang from memory. It is unusual to come upon a man of such accurate memory.*

H. H. F., *Collector*
November 2, 1938

Lord Bakeman

In India lived a noble lord,
His riches were beyond compare.
He was the darling of his parents,
And of their estate an only heir.

He had gold and he had silver
And he had houses of high degree
But still he never could be contented
Until a voyage he had been to sea.

He sailed east and he sailed west
Until he came to the Turkish shore
Where he was taken and put in prison
Where he could neither see nor hear.

For seven long months he lay lamenting,
He laid lamenting in iron bands,
There, happening to see a brisk young lady
Who set him free from his iron chains.

The jailer had one only daughter.
A brisk young lady gay was she.
As she was walking across the floor
She chanced Lord Bakeman for to see.

She stole the keys of her father's prison
And said Lord Bakeman she would set free.
She went unto the prison door
And opened it without delay.

"Have you got gold, or have you got silver?
Have you got houses of high degree?
What will you give the fair lady
If she from bondage will set you free?"

"Yes, I've got gold and I've got silver
And I've got houses of high degree;
I'll give them all to the fair lady
If she from bondage set me free."

"It's not your silver, nor your gold,
Nor yet your houses of high degree.
All that I want to make me happy
And all I crave is your fair body.

"Let us make a bargain and make it strong
For seven long years it shall stand;
You shall not wed no other woman,
Nor I'll not wed no other man."

When seven long years were gone and past,
When seven long years were at an end,
She packed up all her richest clothing,
Saying, "Now I'll go and seek my friend."

She sailed east, she sailed west,
Until she came to the Indian shore
And there she never could be contented
Till for her true love she did enquire.

She did enquire for Lord Bakeman's palace
At every corner of the street;

She enquired after Lord Bakeman's palace
Of every person she chanced to meet.

And when she came to Lord Bakeman's palace
She knocked so loud upon the ring.
There's none so ready as the brisk young porter
To rise and let this fair lady in.

She asked if this was Lord Bakeman's palace,
Or is the lord himself within?
"Yes, yes," replied the brisk young porter,
"He and his bride have just entered in."

She wept, she wept and wrung her hands
Crying, "Alas, I am undone;
I wish I was in my native country
Across the seas there to remain.

"Ask him to send me one ounce of bread
And a bottle of his wine so strong;
And ask him if he's forgot the lady
That set him free from iron chains."

The porter went unto his master
And bowed low upon his knees.
"Arise, arise, my brisk young porter,
And tell me what the matter is."

"There is a lady stands at your gate
And she doth weep most bitterly.
I think she is as fine a creature
As ever I wish my eyes to see.

"She's got more rings on her four fingers
And round her waist has diamond strings;
She's got more gold about her clothing
Than your new bride and all her kin.

"She wants you to send her one ounce of bread
And a bottle of your wine so strong
And asks if you have forgot the lady
That set you free from your prison chains."

He stamped his foot upon the floor;
He broke the table in pieces three.
"Here's adieu to you, my wedded bride,
For this fair lady I will go and see."

Then up spoke his new bride's mother
And she was a lady of high degree.
" 'Tis you have married my only daughter."
"Well, she is none the worse for me.

"But since my fair one has arrived,
A second wedding there shall be.
Your daughter came on a horse and saddle;
She may return in a coach and three."

He took this fair lady by the hand
And led her over the marble stones.
He changed her name from Susannah Fair
And she now is the wife of Lord Bakeman.

He took her by the lily-white hand
And led her through from room to room.
He changed her name from Susannah Fair
And she is called the wife of Lord Bakeman.

B

*This song was known to Mrs. Ella Doten, North Calais,
Vermont, and contributed as she heard it sung when a
child. Mrs. Doten says, "I have written just as I found it in
Mr. Tabor's old song book. An old man by the name of
Wareham Chase, who lived in this place, used to repeat it.
He called it 'Lord Bateman.' He invented the first electric*

motor. It is in the State House at Montpelier." Copied literatim et punctatim. See Version N also.

Lord Bakeman

In India liv'd a noble lord,
His riches was beyond compare,
He was the darling of his parents,
And of their estate an only heir.

He had gold and he had silver,
And he had houses of high degree,
But still he never could be contented,
Until a voyage he had been to sea.

He sailed east, and he sailed west,
Until he came to the Turkish shore,
Where he was taken and put in prison,
Where he could neither see nor hear.

For seven long months he lay lamenting,
He laid lamenting in iron bands,
There happening to see a brisk young lady,
Who set him free from his iron chains.

The jailor had one only daughter,
A brisk young lady gay was she,
As she was walking across the floor,
She chanced Lord Bakeman for to see.

She stole the keys of her father's prison,
And said Lord Bakeman she would set free,
She went unto the prison door,
And opened it without delay.

Have you got gold or have you got silver?
Have you got houses of high degree?
What will you give to the fair Lady,
If she from bondage will set you free?

Yes, I've got gold, and I've got silver,
And I've got houses of high degree,
I'll give them all to the fair lady,
If she from bondage set me free.

It's not your silver nor your gold,
Nor yet your houses of high degree,
All that I want to make me happy,
And all I crave is your fair body.

Let us make a bargain, and make it strong,
For seven long years it shall stand,
You shall not wed no other woman,
Nor I'll not wed no other man.

When seven long years were gone and past,
When seven long years were at an end,
She packed up all her richest clothing,
Saying, now I'll go and seek my friend.

She sailed east, she sailed west,
Until she came to the Indian shore,
And there she never could be contented,
Till for her true love she did enquire.

She did enquire for Lord Bakeman's palace,
At every corner of the street,
She enquired after Lord Bakeman's palace,
Of every person she chanced to meet.

And when she came to Lord Bakeman's palace,
She knock'd so loud upon the ring,
There's none so ready as the brisk young porter,
To rise and let this fair lady in.

She ask'd if this was Lord Bakeman's palace,
Or is the Lord himself within?

Yes, yes, replied the brisk young porter,
He and his bride have just entered in.

She wept, she wept, and rung her hands,
Crying, alas! I am undone;
I wish I was in my native country,
Across the seas there to remain.

Ask him to send me one ounce of bread,
And a bottle of his wine so strong,
And ask him if he's forgot the lady,
That set him free from his iron chains.

The porter went unto his master,
And bowed low upon his knees,
Arise, arise, my brisk young porter,
And tell me what the matter is.

There is a lady stands at your gate,
And she doth weep most bitterly,
I think she is as fine a creature,
As ever I wish my eyes to see.

She's got more rings on her four fingers,
And round her waist has diamond strings,
She's got more gold about her clothing,
Than your new bride and all her kin.

She wants you to send one ounce of bread,
And a bottle of your wine so strong,
And asks if you have forgot the lady,
That set you free from your prison chains.

He stamp'd his foot upon the floor,
He broke the table in pieces three,
Here's adieu to you my wedded bride,
For this fair lady I will go and see.

Then up spoke his new bride's mother,
And she was a lady of high degree,
'Tis you have married my only daughter,
Well she is none the worse for me.

But since my fair one has arrived,
A second wedding there shall be;
Your daughter came on a horse and saddle,
She may return in a coach and three.

He took this fair lady by the hand,
And led her over the marble stones;
He changed her name from Susannah fair,
And she now is the wife of Lord Bakeman.

He took her by her lily white hand,
And led her through from room to room,
He changed her name from Susannah fair,
And she is called the wife of Lord Bakeman.

C

As sung by Arthur Walker of Littleton, Maine.

M. Olney, Collector
August 31, 1942

Lord Bateman

In India there lived a noble lord,
His riches they were beyond compare;
He was the darling of his parents,
Of its estate and its only heir.

For he had gold and he had silver,
He had houses of a high degree,
But still he ne'er could be contented
Until a voyage he had been to sea.

He sail-ded east, he sail-ded west
Until he came to an Indian shore
Where he was taken and put in prison
Where he could neither see nor hear.

Seven long months he lied lamenting,
He lied lamenting in iron bands;
He chanced for to spy a fair young lady,
That sot him free from his prison chains.

Now the jailer had one only daughter,
And a brisk young lady gay was she;
She stole the keys of her father's prison.
She said she would let Lord Bateman free,

Saying, "Have you gold, have you got silver
Or have you houses of a high degree?
What will you give to this fair lady
If she from bondage would set you free?"

"Yes, I've got gold and I've got silver;
I've got houses of a high degree.
I'll give them all to this fair lady,
If she from bondage would set me free."

"It's not your gold nor yet your silver,
Nor yet your houses of a high degree;
It's all I want just to be made happy
And all I crave is your fair bodee.

"Let's get married, now let us talk it strong
For seven long years that it might stand
That you shan't marry no other woman,
Nor I shan't wed no other man."

Oh, several long years was passed and gone;
Several long years were at an end;

Oh, she packed up all of her clothing;
She said she'd go and seek her friend.

She sail-ded east, and she sail-ded west
Until she came to Kentucky shore;
But still she never could be contented,
But for her true love she did inquire.

She did inquire for Lord Bateman's palace,
To every corner of the street;
She did inquire for Lord Bateman's palace,
To every person she chanced to meet.

It's when she got to Lord Bateman's palace,
Oh, she knocked loudly upon the ring;
There's none so ready as the brisk young porter
To arise and let this fair lady in.

She asked if this was Lord Bateman's palace.
"Oh, is the lord himself within?"
"Oh, yes, oh, yes," replied the brisk young porter,
"Him and his new bride they just entered in."

She wept, she wept, and she wrung her hands,
Saying that "At length, I am undone;
I wished I were in my native countree,
Across the seas there to remain.

"You ask him to send me one ounce of bread,
Likewise a bottle of your strongest wine,
And ask him if he does mind that lady
That sot him free from his prison chains."

He stomped his foot upon the floor;
His table he broke it up in three.
"Adieu, adieu to my wedded wife,
To that fair creature I'll go and see."

Oh, the next spoke up was the new bride's mother,
And she was a lady of a high degree.

"Now since you have wed my only daughter,"
"Well, she is none the worse of me.

"Now since I have wed your only daughter,
The second wedding there will be;
If your daughter came in horse or saddle,
She can ride back in a coach by three."

He took her by the lily-white hand,
He led her over the marble stones;
He changed her name from Susanna Fair,
She is now the wife of Lord Bateman here.

D

As sung by Alonzo Lewis of York, Maine. Learned from his father, who was born in York, Maine.

M. Olney, Collector
September 22, 1947

Lord Bateman

In India lived a noble lord
Whose riches was beyond compare;
He was the darling of his parents
And of their[1] estate an only heir.

He had gold, yes, he had silver;
He had houses of high degree,
But still he never could be contented
Till a voyage he went to sea.

He sailed east, and he sailed west
Until he came to the Indie shore,
Where he was taken and put in prison
Where he could neither see nor hear.

The jailer had one lovely daughter,
A brisk young lady, gay was she.

[1] Pronounced *ther.*

As she was a-walking across the floor
She chanced Lord Bateman's face to see,

Saying, "Have you got gold, have you got silver,
Have you got houses of high degree?
What will you give to the lady fair
If she from bondage will set you free?"

"Yes, I've got gold, yes, I've got silver,
I've got houses of high degree;
I will give them all to the lady fair
If she from bondage will set me free."

She stole the keys of her father's prison
And opened it without delay,
"Now let's make a bargain, and make it strong
For seven long years that it will stand
And you'll not wed with no other woman,
And I'll not wed with no other man."

When seven long years was over and past
And seven long years was at an end,
'Tis, "I'll pick up all of my richest clothing;
Now I will go and seek my friend."

She sailed east, she sailed west
Until she came to the Indie shore,
Where she never could be contented
Till for Lord Bateman she did inquire.

She inquired for Lord Bateman's palace
To every corner of the street.
She inquired for Lord Bateman's palace
To every person she chanced to meet,

Until she came to Lord Bateman's palace.
She knocked so loud upon the ring;

There was none so ready as the brisk young porter
To rise and let this fair one in,

Saying, "Is this Lord Bateman's palace?
And is the Lord himself within?"
"Yes, yes," the brisk young porter,
"He and his bride have just entered in."

"Tell him to send me one ounce of bread
And a bottle of his wine so strong
And ask him if he has forgot that lady
That sot him free from his iron chains."

The porter went unto the master;
He bowed so low upon his knees.
"Arise, arise, my brisk young porter,
Come and tell to me what the matter is."

"There is a young lady stands at your gate
And she does weep most bitterly;
I think she is the finest creature
That ever my two eyes did see.

"She wants you to send her one ounce of bread
And a bottle of your wine so strong
And ask you if you've forgot that lady
That sot you free from your iron chains."

He stamped his foot upon the floor;
He split the table in pieces three,
Saying, "Since my new one has arrived
A second wedding there will be!"

He took his new bride by the hand;
He led her from room to room;
He changed her name from Susanna Fair,
And now she's the wife of Lord Bateman.

E

As sung by Mrs. Belle Richards of Colebrook, New Hampshire.

M. Olney, Collector
July 21, 1943

Lord Bateman

In India there lived a noble lord.
His riches were beyond compare.
He was the darling of his parents
And of their estate an only heir.
He had gold and he had silver
And he had houses of high degree
But still he never could be contented
Until a voyage he had been to sea.

He sailed east and he sailed west
Until he came to the Turkey shore
Where he was taken and put in prison
Where he could neither see nor hear.
For seven long months he lay lamenting,
He lay lamenting in iron bands.
There happened to see a brisk young lady
Who set him free from his iron chains.

The jailer had one only daughter;
A brisk young lady gay was she.
As she was walking across the floor
She chanced Lord Bateman for to see.
She stole the keys of her father's prison
And said Lord Bateman she would set free.
She went unto the prison door
And opened it without delay.

"Have you got gold or have you got silver?
Have you got houses of high degree?

What will you give the fair young lady
If she from bondage will set you free?"

"Yes, I've got gold and I've got silver
And I've got houses of high degree.
I'll give them all to the fair lady
If she from bondage sets me free."
"It's not your silver, nor your gold,
Nor yet your houses of high degree.
All that I want to make me happy
And all that I crave is your fair bodee.

"Let us make a bargain and make it strong;
For seven long years it shall stand:
You shall not wed no other woman
Nor I'll not wed no other man."

When seven long years were gone and past,
When seven long years were at an end,
She packed up all her richest clothing,
Saying, "Now, I'll go and seek my friend."

She sailed east, she sailed west
Until she came to the Indian shore
And now she never could be contented
Till for her true love she did enquire.
She did enquire for Lord Bateman's palace
At every corner of the street.
She enquired after Lord Bateman's palace
Of every person she chanced to meet.

When she came to Lord Bateman's palace
She knocked so loud upon the ring;
There's none so ready as the brisk young porter
To arise and let this fair lady in.
She asked if this was Lord Bateman's palace
Or is the Lord himself within.

"Yes, yes," replied the brisk young porter,
"He and his bride have just entered in."

"Ask him to send me one ounce of bread
And a bottle of his wine so strong
And ask him if he forgot the lady
That set him free from his prison chains."

The porter went unto his master
And bowed low upon his knee.
"Arise, arise, my brisk young porter,
And tell me what the matter is."
"There is a lady stands at your gate
And she does weep most bitterly.
I think she is as fine a creature
As ever I wish my eyes to see.

"She's got more rings on her four fingers
And round her waist the diamonds cling.
She's got more gold about her clothing
Than your new bride and all her kin.

"She wants you to send her one ounce of bread
And a bottle of your wine so strong
And ask if you have forgot the lady
That set you free from your prison chains."
He struck his fist upon the table.
He broke the table in pieces three,
Saying, "I'll forsake my land and living
If Susannah Frye has got to see."

Then up spoke his new bride's mother,
Saying such a thing was never known—
To marry a bride all in the morning,
Another one in the afternoon.

Then up spake this noble lord.
"Your daughter is none the worse for me.
She came here with a horse and saddle.
She is going home with my coach and three."

He took this fair lady by the hand
And led her over the marble stone.
He changed her name from Susannah Fair
And now she is the wife of Lord Bateman.

He took her by the lily-white hand
And led her through from room to room.
He changed her name from Susannah Fair
And she is called the wife of Lord Bateman.

F

*Asa Davis of Milton, Vermont, sang this song as learned
from his grandfather, Charles Atkins, and from his father,
Joel Davis of Duxbury, Vermont. His father owned the
book* Popular Songs *and gave tunes to many there. In July,
1946, and again for an L-P record in 1953, Mr. Davis resang the song with the changes noted below. Printed in*
Ballads Migrant in New England, *54.*

H. H. F., Collector
June 23, 1939

Structure: A B¹ B² Bª (2,2,2,2); Rhythm E; Contour: arc;
Scale: major

t.c. C.

For melodic relationship see SSC, 104; RO 1, 81; BES, 106
(very close); Sharp 1, 80(C).

Lord Bakeman

Lord Bakeman

In India lived a noble lord
Whose riches were beyond compare;
He was the darling of his parents
And of his estate the only heir.

Oh, he had gold and he had silver
And he had houses of high degree
But he could never be contented
Until a voyage he had been to sea.

He sail-ed east, he sail-ed west
Until he came to the Turkey shore.
There he was taken and put in prison
Where he could neither see nor hear.

For seven long months he lay lamenting,
He lay lamenting in iron chains.
There happened to be a brisk young lady
Who released him out of his iron bands.

The jailer had an only daughter,
A brisk young lady gay was she;

As she was walking across the floor
She chanced Lord Bakeman for to see.

She stole the keys of her father's prison
And vowed Lord Bakeman she would set free,
She went unto the prison door
And opened it without delay.

"Have you got gold, have you got silver,
And have you houses of high degree?
What will you give to the ladee fay-er
If she from bondage will set you free?"

"Yes, I've got gold and I've got silver
And I have houses of high degree
And I'll give them all to the fair lady
If she from bondage will set me free."

"I do not want your gold nor silver
Nor your houses of high degree.
What all I want for to make me happy
And all I crave is your fair bodee.

"Let us make a bargain and make it strong—
For seven long years it shall stand:
You shall not marry no other woman
And I'll not marry no other man."

When seven long years had gone and passed,
When seven long years were at an end,
She packed up all her rich gay clothing,
Saying, "Now I'll go and seek a friend."

She sail-ed east, she sail-ed west
Until she came to the Indian shore.
There she could never be contented
Until Lord Bakeman she did enquire.

She enquired for Lord Bakeman's palace
At every corner of the street.

She did enquire of Lord Bakeman's palace
Of every person she chanced to meet.

And when she came to Lord Bakeman's palace
She knocked so loud upon the ring;
There was none so ready as the brisk young porter
To arise and let this fair lady in.

"Oh, is this Lord Bakeman's palace
And is the Lord himself within?"
"Oh, yes," cries the brisk young porter,
"He and his new bride has just entered in."

She wept, she wept and she wrung her hands,
Crying, "I am undone.
I wish't I was in my native countree,
Across the seas there to remain.

"Tell him to send me an ounce of bread
And a bottle of his wine so strong
And ask him if he has forgot the lady
That released him out of his iron band."

The porter went unto his master;
He rapped so loud upon the ring.[1]
"Arise, my brisk young porter,[2]
And tell me what the matter is."

"There is a lady stands at your gate
And she does weep so bitterly.
I think she is the finest creature
That ever I chanced my eyes to see.

"She's got more rings on her four fingers
And on her wrist are diamond bands.

[1] In 1946 and in 1953 this line was "He knelt so long upon one knee."
[2] In 1946 and in 1953 this line begins "Arise, arise . . ."

She got more gold about her clothing
Than your bride and all her kin.

"She wants you to send her an ounce of bread
And a bottle of your wine so strong
And ask you if you have forgot the lady
That released you out of your iron band."

He jumped into the middle of the floor.
He smashed the table in pieces three.
"You came here in a horse and saddle,
You may ride home in a coach and three."

[*The previous stanzas Mr. Davis sang from memory. The
following he read from* Popular Songs.] [3]

Then up spoke his new bride's mother,
And she was a lady of high degree,
'Tis you have married my only daughter,
Well she is none the worse for me.

But since my fair one has arrived,
A second wedding there shall be;
Your daughter came on a horse and saddle,
She may return in a coach and three.

He took this fair lady by the hand,
And led her over the marble stones;
He changed her name from Suzannah fair,
And she now is the wife of Lord Bakeman.

He took her by her lily white hand,
And led her through from room to room,
He changed her name from Suzannah fair,[4]
And she is called the wife of Lord Bakeman.

[3] In 1946 and in 1953 these lines were sung with the rest, without reference
to the book.
[4] In 1946 and in 1953 the girl is called Suzannah Freeman. The Lord
is called Bateman in 1946.

G

As sung by J. E. Shepard, of Baltimore, Vermont, to H. H. F. and Phillips Barry, as learned from his mother, a native of Ireland.

H. H. F., *Collector*
July 9, 1933

Lord Bakeman

In India lived a noble lord.
His riches were beyond compare.
He was the darling of his parents,
An only son and only heir.

He had gold and he had silver
And he had houses of high degree.
Still he could never be contented
Until a voyage he had been to sea.

He sailed east and he sailed west.
He sailed till he came to the Turkey shore.
There he was taken and put in prison
Where he could neither see nor hear no more.

For seven long months he laid lamenting,
He laid lamenting in iron chains
Until a lady chanced to see him
Which set him free from his iron bonds.

The jailer had one only daughter,
A brisk young lady gay was she.
As she was going acrost the room
She chanced Lord Bakeman for to see.

"Have you got gold, have you got silver,
Have you got houses of high degree?
What will you give to this fair lady
If from your bondage will set you free?"

"Yes, I've got gold and I've got silver
And I've got houses of high degree.
I'll give it all to thee, fair lady,
If from my bondage you'll set me free."

"Let us make a bargain and make it strong—
For seven long years we will let it stand
That you will wed with no other woman
And I will wed with no other man."

When seven long years was passed and gone,
When seven long years was at an end,
She picked up all her richest clothing,
Saying, "Now I'll go and seek my friend."

She sailed east, she sailed west,
Sailed till she came to India's shore.
There she could never be contented
Until Lord Bakeman she did enquire.

She enquired for Lord Bakeman's palace
On every corner of the street;
She enquired for Lord Bakeman's palace
Of every person that she met.

When she came to Lord Bakeman's palace
She knocked so loud upon the ring;
There was no one so ready as the brisk young porter
To rise and let this lady in.

She enquired if this was Lord Bakeman's palace
And if the Lord himself was in.
"Oh yes," replied the brisk young porter,
"Him and his new bride has just came in."

She wept, she wept, she wrung her hands,
Crying, "Alas, I am undone.

I wish't I was in my native country
Across the seas where I came from.

"Tell him to send me one ounce of bread
And a bottle of his wine so strong.
Ask him if he's forgot the lady
That set him free from his iron bonds."

The porter went unto the master;
He bowed himself upon his knee.
"Oh, arise, arise, my brisk young porter,
And tell me what the matter is."

"There is a lady at your gate
And she doth weep most bitterlee.
I think she is as fair a lady
As ever I wish my eyes to see.

"She's got more rings on her forefinger
And about her waist there's diamonds strung.
She's got more gold about her clothing
Than your new bride and all her kin.

"She wants you to send her one ounce of bread
And a bottle of your wine so strong.
She enquired if you had forgotten the lady
That set you free from his iron bonds."

He stamped his foot, he raged aloud,
He broke the table in pieces three.
"Adieu, adieu, my fair wedded bride,
This fair lady I will go and see."

Then up and spoke the new bride's mother.
She was a lady of high degree.
"Since you've married my only daughter,
And she's none the worse for thee."

"Since I married your only daughter,
A second wedding there shall be.
Your daughter came in horse and saddle
And can return in a coach and three."

He took her by the lily-white hand.
He led her o'er the marble stone.
He changed her name from Susanah Fair.
She's called the wife of Lord Bakeman.

H

*Sung by Josiah Samuel Kennison of Townshend, Vermont.
Learned from the singer's mother, Mrs. Sophronia (Codding) Kennison, in Johnson, Vermont. Mr. Kennison's
grandfather, Russell Codding, came from England with
three brothers and settled Codding's Hollow in Johnson.
On November 27, 1942, Mr. Kennison sang this ballad for
Miss Marguerite Olney in practically identical form. Printed
in* Vermont Folk-Songs & Ballads, *204. The last two lines
of each stanza are repeated.*

George Brown, Collector
August 23, 1930

Structure: A B C^b A C^b A (2,2,2,2,2,2); Rhythm E; Contour:
arc; Scale: Mixolydian

t.c. D.

For mel. rel. see BES, 106; RO 1, 81; SSC, 104.

Lord Bakeman

Lord Bakeman, he was a noble lord
And he had riches of high degree,
But never could he be contented
Until a voyage he had been to sea.

Lord Bakeman

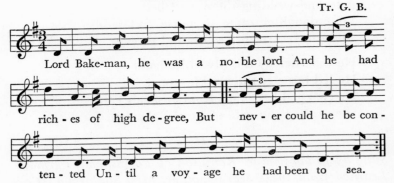

He sail-ed east and he sail-ed west
Until he came to the Turkey shore,
And there he was taken and put in prison
Where he could neither see nor hear.

Seven long months he lie lamented,[1]
He lie lamented in iron bonds,
Until he spied a calm-eyed damsel [2]
Who set him free from his iron bonds.

She was walking across the floor;
She chanced Lord Bakeman for to see;
She stole the keys of her father's prison,
Saying, "Now Lord Bakeman I'll set free.

"Have you got gold, have you got silver,
Or have you houses of high degree?
And what will you give to this fair lady
If she from bondage will set you free?"

"Yes, I've got gold and I've got silver,
And I've got houses of high degree;

[1] In 1942 "lay-menting" for "lamented."
[2] In 1942 "com-lie" for "calm-eyed."

All these I'll give to this fair lady
If she from bondage will set me free."

"I want none of your gold nor silver
Nor none of your houses of high degree;
But all I ask to make me happy
For all I crave is your fair body.

"Let us make a bargain and make it strong,
And seven long years that it shall stand,
That you shan't wed no other woman
Nor I shan't wed no other man."

When seven long years were gone and passed,
And seven long years were at an end,
She then packed up all her richest clothing,
Saying, "Now I'll go to seek my friend."

She sail-ed east and she sail-ed west,
Until she came to the Indee shore,
And there she inquired for Lord Bakeman's palace
In every corner of the street.
And there she inquired for Lord Bakeman's palace
To every one she chanced to meet.

"Is this Lord Bakeman's palace,
Or is the Lord himself within?"
"Yes, yes, oh yes," cries the brisk young porter,
"He and his new bride has just entered in."

Then she did wring her lily-white hands,
And she did weep most bitterly,
Saying, "I wish I was back across the ocean
In my own country for to stay.

"Go ask Lord Bakeman to send me one ounce of bread
And a bottle of his wine so strong,

And ask if he has forgotten the lady
Who set him free from his iron bonds."

Away, away ran the brisk young porter
And down upon his bended knees.
"Arise, arise, my brisk young porter,
And tell me what the matter is."

"There stands a lady at your gate
And she doth weep most bitterly.
I think she is the fairest lady
That ever my eyes could wish to see.

"She has a ring on every finger
And on her forefinger she has three;
She's got more gold about her clothing
Than your new bride and all her kin.

"She sent me for an ounce of bread
And a bottle of your wine so strong,
And to ask if you'd forgotten the lady
Who set you free from your iron bonds." [3]

He stamped his foot on the marble floor;
He split the table in pieces three,
Saying, "Adieu, adieu, to the wedded bride,[4]
And this fair lady I'll go to see."

Then up steps the new bride's mother,
She being a lady of high degree,
Saying, "You've married my only daughter
And she's a lady of high degree.
I wish to God that Silky Friar
Had died before she'd crossed the sea."

[3] In 1942 this line was "Who from bondage has set you free."
[4] In 1942 this line was "Saying, 'Adieu, adieu to the new wedded bride . . .'"

"Yes, I married your only daughter
But she is none the worse for me;
She came to me on a horse and saddle;
She shall go back in a coach so free." [5]

He took her by her lily-white hand
And led her across the marble floor.
He changed her name from Silky Friar;
She's now the wife of Lord Bakeman.

I

As copied by Miss Barbara Pierce from a version handwritten by her mother (deceased), Mrs. W. E. Pierce of North Shrewsbury, Vermont, who used to sing the Lord Bateman verses. On July 14, 1932, she sang the second verse to Mrs. Flanders to the first tune given below. In 1953 her daughter Marjorie gave the tune as she remembered it from her mother's singing.

H. H. F., Collector
July, 1953

Structure: A¹ A² B C (2,2,2,2); Rhythm E; Contour: descending; Scale: anhemitonic pentatonic

t.c. G.

For mel. rel. see Sharp 1, 81(E), distant.

Lord Bateman

In India lived a noble lord,
And he was a man of high degree.
He vowed he'd never be contented
Until a voyage he'd made to sea.

[5] In 1942 this line was "She shall go back in a coach and three."

Tr. M. O.

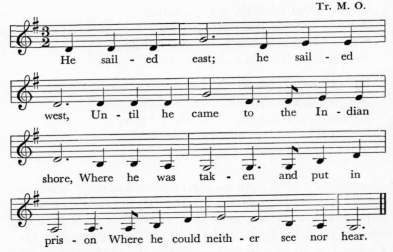

He sail-ed east; he sail-ed west, Un-til he came to the In-dian shore, Where he was tak-en and put in pris-on Where he could neith-er see nor hear.

He sail-ed east and he sail-ed west
Until he came unto Turkey,
Where he was taken and put in prison
Where he could neither hear nor see.[1]

The jailer had one only daughter;
And she was a lady of high degree.
She stole the keys to her father's prison
And vowed she'd set Lord Bateman free.

"Oh, I've got houses and I've got lands,
And I've got titles of high degree.

Structure: A B^1 B^2 C (2,2,2,2); Rhythm E; Contour: arc;
Scale: hexatonic—but leading tone B appears only once

t.c. C.

For mel. rel. see SSC, 104; BES, 106.

[1] This stanza with the words "to the Indian shore" in place of "unto Turkey" was sung to Mrs. Flanders by Mrs. Pierce on July 14, 1932.

Lord Bateman

Tr. M. O.

In In-dia lived a no-ble lord, And he was a man of high de-gree. He vowed he'd nev-er be con-tent-ed Un-til a voy-age he'd made to sea.

I'll give them all to the fair young lady
Who will from bondage set me free."

" 'Tis not your silver, 'tis not your gold,
Nor yet your titles of high degree.

All that I want to make me happy,
All that I crave is your fair bod-y."

"Let us make a bargain and make it strong:
For seven long years it shall stand,
If you will wed no other woman,
Then I will wed no other man."

When seven long years were gone and past,
When seven long years were at an end,
She packed up all her richest clothing
And said, "Now I'll go and seek my friend."

She sailed east and she sailed west
Until she came to the India shore
.   .   .   .
And for Lord Bateman she did inquire.

She did inquire for Lord Bateman's palace
At every corner of the street.
She did inquire for Lord Bateman's palace
From everyone she chanced to meet.

And when she came to Lord Bateman's palace,
She knocked so loud upon the door
.   .   .   .
.   .   .   .

She asked, "Is this Lord Bateman's palace,
And is the Lord himself within?"
"Yes, yes," replied the brisk young porter,
"He and his bride have just entered in."

She wept and wept and wrung her hands
Saying, "Alas, I am undone.
I wish I was in my native country,
My native land there to remain.

"Ask him to send me one ounce of bread,
And a bottle of his wine so strong.
And ask if he has forgot the lady
Who set him free from his iron bonds."

The porter went unto his master
And bowed so low upon his knee.
"Arise, arise my brisk young porter,
And tell me what the matter is.

"What news, what news, my brisk young porter,
What news, what news have you brought unto me?"
.   .   .   .
.   .   .   .

"There is a lady stands at your gate,
And she doth weep most bitterly.
I think she is the fairest creature
That ever my two eyes did see.

"She has got rings on every finger (her four fingers)
And 'round her neck has diamond strings, (And on one of
        them she has got three)
She has more gold about her middle
Than your new bride and all her kin.

"She asks you to send her one ounce of bread
And a bottle of your wine so strong
And asks if you have forgot the lady
Who set you free from your iron bonds."

J

As sung by Mrs. W. B. Morton of Groton, Vermont.

H. H. F., *Collector*
October 19, 1937

Structure: A¹ B A² B (2,2,2,2); Rhythm E; Contour: each
line an arc; Scale: hexatonic

t.c. D. Note the small range (major sixth).

For mel. rel. see RO 1, 83, 86; BES, 119; Bruno Nettl, in
Acta Musicologica (1955), 83, first song.

Lord Bateman

Tr. M. O.

Lord Bateman

In India lived a noble lord.
His riches were beyond compare.
He was the darling of his parents
And of their estate an only heir.

He had gold and he had silver;
He had houses of high degree,
But he could not be contented
Until a voyage he went to sea.

He sailed east and he sailed west,
He sailed till he came to an Indian shore

Where he was taken and put in prison
Where he could neither see nor hear.

For seven long months he lay lamenting,
He laid lamenting in iron bands,
There happening to see a brisk young lady
Who set him free from his iron chains.

The jailer had one only daughter,
A brisk young lady, gay was she;
As she was walking across the floor,
She chanced Lord Bateman for to see.

She stole the keys of her father's prison
And said Lord Bateman she would set free.
She went unto the prison door
And opened it without delay.

"Have you got gold or have you got silver?
Have you got houses of high degree?
What will you give to the fair young lady
If she from bondage will set you free?"

"Yes, I've got gold, and I've got silver,
And I've got houses of high degree.
I'll give them all to the fair young lady,
If she from bondage set me free."

"It's not your silver nor your gold,
Nor yet your houses of high degree;
All that I want to make me happy
And all I crave is your fair body."

K

*Mrs. W. L. Bryant of Springfield, Vermont, loaned the
Archive an old booklet* Uncle Franks' Series *published by*

McLoughlin Bros., 24 Beekman, containing "Lord Bate-man."

                                        H. H. F., Collector
                                        1930's

Lord Bateman

Lord Bateman he was a noble lord,
A noble lord of high degree,
He shipped himself on board a ship,
Some foreign country he would go see.

He sailed East, and he sailed West,
Until he came to proud Turkey,
Where he was taken and put to prison,
Until his life was almost weary.

And in this prison there grew a tree,
It grew so stout and strong,
Where he was chained by the middle,
Until his life was almost gone.

This Turk he had one only daughter,
The fairest creature my eyes did see,
She stole the keys of her father's prison,
And said Lord Bateman she would set free.

Have you got houses have you got lands,
Or does Northumberland belong to thee,
What would you give to the fair young lady
That out of prison would set you free.

I have got houses, I have got lands,
And half Northumberland belongs to me,
I'll give it all to the fair young lady,
That out of prison would set me free.

O then she took him to her father's hall,
And gave to him the best of wine,

And every health she drank unto him,
I wish Lord Bateman that you were mine.

Now in seven years I'll make a vow,
And seven years I'll keep it strong,
If you'll wed with no other woman,
I will wed with no other man.

O then she took him to her father's harbour
And gave to him a ship of fame,
Farewell farewell to you Lord Bateman,
I'm afraid I ne'er shall see you again.

Now seven long years are gone and past,
And fourteen days well known to thee,
She packed up all her gay clothing,
And said Lord Bateman she would go see.

But when she came to Lord Bateman's castle
So boldly she rang the bell,
Who's there, who's there cry'd the proud porter
Who's there come tell unto me.

O is this Lord Bateman's castle,
Or is his Lordship here within,
O yes, O yes, cried the young porter
He's just now taken his new bride in.

O tell him to send me a slice of bread,
And a bottle of the best of wine,
And not forgetting the fair young lady,
Who did release him when close confin'd.

Away away went this young proud porter,
Away away, and away went he,
Until he came to Lord Bateman's chamber,
Down on his bended knees fell he.

What news, what news, my proud young porter
What news hast thou brought unto me,

There is the fairest of all young creatures,
That e'er my two eyes did see.

She has got rings on every finger,
And round one of them she has got three,
And as much gay clothing round her middle
As would buy all Northumberland.

She bids you send her a slice of bread,
And a bottle of the best of wine,
And not forgetting the fair young lady,
Who did release you when close confin'd.

Lord Bateman he then in a passion flew,
And broke his sword in splinters three,
Saying I will give all my father's riches,
That if Sophia has crossed the sea.

Then up spoke the young bride's mother,
Who never was heard to speak so free,
You'll not forget my only daughter,
That if Sophia has crossed the sea.

I own I made a bride of your daughter,
She's neither the better nor worse for me
She came to me with her horse and saddle,
She may go back in her coach and three.

Lord Bateman prepared another marriage,
With both their hearts so full of glee,
I'll range no more in foreign countries,
Now since Sophia has crossed the sea.

L

The following lines were furnished by Mrs. Lena Rich, postmistress of Belvidere, Vermont. When a young school-girl, Mrs. Rich with the help of her aunt compiled a book of poetry, folk songs, and paper-clippings. The poetry and

*folk songs were items which had been recited and sung in
and around Belvidere. The paper-clippings, taken from a
newspaper, related for the most part "events of the time."*

*As Mrs. Rich was unable to recall the tune to this ballad,
I hummed three different melodies. Mrs. Rich without
hesitation selected the melody she associated with this ballad.
It was the air generally used by the traditional Vermont
folk singer.*

Copied literatim et punctatim.

M. Olney, Collector
November 18, 1954

Lord Bateman

Lord Bateman was a noble lord.
A noble lord of high degree;
He shipped himself on board of a ship,
Some foreign country for to see.

He sailed east, he sailed west
Until he came unto Turkey
When he was taken and put in prison
Until his life was quite weary

In this prison there grew a tree
It grew so very stout and strong
And he was chained by the middle
Until his life was almost gone.

The Turk he had one only daughter
The fairest creature eye ere did see;
She stole the keys of her father's prison
And said she'd set Lord Bateman free.

"Have you got houses, have you got lands
And does Northumberland belong to thee?
And what would you give to the fair young lady
Who out of prison would set you free?"

Oh, I've got houses and I've got lands
And half Northumberland belongs to me,
I'd give it all to the fair young lady
If out of prison would set me free."

She took him then to her father's palace,
And gave to him the best of wine.
And every health that she drank unto him,
Was, "I wish Lord Bateman, that you were mine!"

For seven long years I'll make a vow—
And seven long years I'll keep it strong
If you will wed no other woman
Then I'll wed no other man.

Then she took him to her father's harbour
And gave to him a ship of fame,
"Farewell, farewell, to you Lord Bateman,
I fear I'll n'er see you again!"

When seven long years were gone and past
And fourteen days well known to me
She packed up her gold and clothing
And said Lord Bateman she would see.

When she came to Lord Bateman's castle,
So boldly there she rang the bell,
"Who's there, who's there." cried the young proud porter,
"Who's there, who's there, unto me tell."

"Oh, is this Lord Bateman's castle?
And is his lordship here within?"
"Oh, yes, oh, yes," cried the proud young porter.
"He has just now taken his new bride in."

"Tell him to send me a slice of cake
And a bottle of his best wine
And not to forget the fair young lady
That did release him when close confined."

Away, away went this proud young porter,
Away, away, away went he
Until he came to Lord Bateman's castle
When on his bended knees fell he.

"What news, what news, my proud young porter.
"What news, what news have you brought to me?"
Oh, there is the fairest of all young ladies
That ever my two eyes did see.

She's got rings on every finger,
And on one of them she has got three,
And she's got as much gold around her middle
As would buy Northumberland of thee.

"She tells you to send her a slice of cake
And a bottle of your best wine
And not to forget the fair young lady
That did release you when close confined."

Lord Bateman in a passion flew.
He broke his sword in splinters three
"To you I will give all my father's riches
Now that Sophia has crossed the sea."

Then up spoke the young bride's mother,
Who never was heard to speak so free
"Don't you forget my only daughter
Although Sophia has crossed the sea."

"I own I've made a bride of your daughter
She's none the better or worse for me,
She came to me on a horse and saddle
She may return in a coach and three."

Then another marriage was prepared,
With both their hearts so full of glee,
"I'll rove no more to foreign countries
Since Sophia has crossed the sea for me."

M

Orlon Merrill sang this to H. H. F. and Phillips Barry in Charlestown, New Hampshire. Printed in the Springfield, Mass., Republican, *February 14, 1932.*

H. H. F., *Collector*
Mid-October, 1931

Lord Bakeman

Lord Bakeman, being a noble lord,
A noble lord of high degree,
He rigged himself on board a ship
Some foreign country to go and see.

He sail-ed east, he sail-ed west
Until he came to a Turkish shore
And there he was taken and put in prison
For six or eight long months or more.

All in this prison grew a tree
And it did grow both stout and strong
And he was chain-ed up by the middle
Until his life was nearly gone.

This Turkish, having an only daughter,
As fair a creature as your two eyes did see,
She stole the key from her father's prison
And swore Lord Bakeman she would see.

"Have you got houses? Have you got land
Or how much of Northumberlie belongs to thee
Or what would thou give to a fair young lady
Which out of prison would set you free?"

"Yes, I've got houses and I've got land
And half of Northumberlie belongs to me.
I'd give it all to any fair young lady,
If out of prison would set me free."

She took him to her father's palace
And she treated him on the best of wine
And every health she drank unto him,
"I wish, Lord Bakeman, you was mine.

"Let's make a vow and make it strong

. . . .

If you will not wed no other woman
I will not wed no other man."

Then she took him to her father's harbor.
She rigged him out on a ship of fame,
Saying, "Fare you well, fare you well, Lord Bakeman.
I fear I ne'er shall see you again."

When seven years had gone past
And seven more, most speedily
She pack-ed up all her gay gold clothing
And swore Lord Bakeman she would go and see.

She sail-ed east, she sail-ed west
Until she came to Lord Bakeman's castle

. . . .

. . . .

. . . .

So loudly there she rang the bell.
"Who's here, who's here?" cried the young proud porter.
"Who's here, who's here? To me now tell."

"Is this Lord Bakeman's castle
Or is His Lordship within?"
"Oh yes, Oh yes," cried the young proud porter,
"He has just now taken a young bride."

"Go tell him to send me a slice of bread
And a bottle of his best wine
And to not forget that fair young lady
That did release him from a close confine."

"Oh, you understand the finest lady
That ever your two eyes did see.
She has got rings on every finger
And on one of them she has got three.

"She has as much gay gold about her clothing
As purchased half of Northumberlie.
She wants you to send her a slice of your bread
And a bottle of your best of wine.

"She wants you to see her
. . . .
And to not forget that fair young lady
That did release you from close confine."

Lord Bakeman in a passion flew.
He broke his sword in splinters three,
Saying, "I care no more, no more for riches
Since that bright youth has crossed the sea."

Then up speaks this young bride's mother
Which never was known to speak so free,
"You've made a bride all of my daughter.
What need you further with she?"

"If I've made a bride all of your daughter,
She's none the better nor the worse for me.
She came to me with a horse and saddle;
She may go back with a coach and three."

Then he took his fair lady by the lily-white hand.
He led her through, from room to room,
And he changed her name from Susannah Fair
To be the wife of Lord Bakeman Esquire.

N

*Copied from a printed copy in a scrapbook of broadsides
originally belonging to the late Ella Doten of North Calais,*

Vermont. Mrs. Lucia Haskins, her daughter, had no knowl-
edge of its origin or whether this version was ever sung by
her mother. It is not like the version which Mrs. Doten
formerly had sung for Mrs. Flanders. (See B above.)

M. Olney, Collector
July 23, 1941

Lord Bateman

Lord Bateman was a noble lord,
A noble lord of high degree;
He shipped on board a ship,
Some foreign countries he would see.

He sail-ed east, he sail-ed west
Until he came to Turkey,
Where he was taken and put in prison
Until his life was quite weary.

In this prison there grew a tree,
It grew so very stout and strong;
And he was chained by the middle,
Until his life was almost gone.

The Turk, he had one only daughter,
The fairest creature eye e're did see;
She stole the keys of her father's prison,
And said she'd set Lord Bateman free.

"Have you got houses, have you got lands,
Or does Northumberland belong to thee?
And what would you give to the fair young lady,
Who out of prison would set you free?"

"Oh, I've got houses, and I've got lands,
And half Northumberland belongs to me:
And I'd give it all to the fair young lady
That out of prison would set me free."

"For seven long years I'll make a vow,
And seven long years I'll keep it strong;
If you will wed no other woman,
I will wed no other man."

Then she took him to her father's harbour
And gave him a ship of fame;
"Farewell, farewell to you Lord Bateman,
I fear I shall never see you again."

When seven long years were gone and past,
And fourteen days, well known to me;
She packed up her gay gold and clothing,
And said Lord Bateman she would see.

When she came to Lord Bateman's castle,
So boldly there she rang the bell;
"Who's there, who's there?" cried the young proud porter,
"Who's there, who's there? unto me tell."

"O is this Lord Bateman's castle?
And is his lordship here within?"
"O yes, O yes" cried the proud young porter;
"He has just now taken his young bride in."

"Tell him to send me a slice of cake
And a bottle of the best wine,
And not to forget the fair young lady
That did release him when close confined."

Away, away went this proud young porter,
Away, away, away went he,
Until he came unto Lord Bateman,
When on his bended knee fell he.

"What news, what news, my proud young porter,
What news, what news have you brought unto me?"
"O, there is the fairest of young ladies
That ever my two eyes did see."

"She has got rings on every finger
And on one of them she has got three,
And she has got as much gold around her middle
As would buy Northumberland of thee."

"She tells you to send her a slice of cake
And a bottle of the best wine,
And not to forget the fair young lady
That did release you when close confined."

Lord Bateman in a passion flew,
He broke his sword in splinters three;
"I'll give all my father's wealth and riches
Now, if Sophia has crossed the sea."

Then up spoke his young bride's mother,
Who never was heard to speak so free;
"Don't you forget my only daughter,
Although Sophia has crossed the sea."

"I own I made a bride of your daughter,
She's none the better or worse by me;
She came to me on a horse and saddle
And she may go back in a coach and three."

Then another marriage was prepared
With both their hearts so full of glee;
"I'll range no more to foreign countries
Since Sophia has crossed the sea."

O

*As sung by Mrs. Grant Coville of Pittsburg, New Hampshire
(retake by M. Olney). Mrs. Coville gave H. H. F. the words
to this ballad at an earlier date, possibly 1939.*

*Retake, M. Olney
September 5, 1941*

Structure: A B¹ B² C (2,2,2,2); Rhythm E; Contour: arc;
Scale: major or Mixolydian

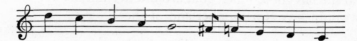

t.c. D. C and C-sharp seem here to be two distinct tones.
Note also the sequencelike treatment.

For mel. rel. see BES, 119; Bruno Nettl, in *Acta Musicologica* (1955), 83, first song.

Lord Bateman

Tr. M. O.

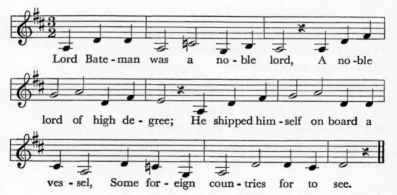

Lord Bateman

Lord Bateman was a noble lord,
A noble lord of high degree;
He shipped himself on board a vessel,
Some foreign countries for to see.

He sail-ed east, he sail-ed west,
Until he came to India's shore
Where he was taken and bound in irons,
Until his life was quite weary.

And in this prison there grew a tree,
And there it grew so strong and stout.
They took and chained him 'round his middle
Until his life was nearly gone.

Now this Turk had an only daughter,
As fair as any two eyes did see;
She stole the keys of her father's prison
And swore Lord Bateman she would go and see.

"Lord Bateman, have you got houses and land,
Or does Northumberlee belong to thee?
What would you give to any fair young lady
Who out of prison could set you free?"

"Oh, I have houses, I have lands,
And half of Northumberlee belongs to me;
I'd give it all to any fair young lady,
Who out of prison would set me free."

Then she took him to her father's cellar
And gave to him the best of wine;
And every health she drank unto him,
"I wish, Lord Bateman, that you were mine!"

Then they made a vow for seven long years,
That seven long years they would keep strong,
That he would marry no other woman
And she would marry no other man.

Then she took him to her father's harbour
And fit him out on a ship of fame;
"Fare you well, fare you well, fare you well, Lord Bateman,
I fear I ne'er shall see you again."

When seven long years had gone and past
And seven more most speedily,
She pick-ed up all her gay gold clothing
And swore Lord Bateman she would go and see.

She sail-ed east, she sail-ed west
Until she came to Lord Bateman's castle;
So promptly then she rang the bell

.   .   .   .

"Who's here, who's here?" cried the young proud porter,
"Who's here, who's here? Unto me now tell."

.   .   .   .

.   .   .   .

"Is this Lord Bateman's castle
Or is His Lordship within?"
"Oh yes, oh yes," cries the young proud porter,
"But he's just now taken a young bride in."

"Go tell him to send me a slice of bread
And a bottle of his best of wine
And to not forget that fair young lady
Who did release him from close confine."

"Here yonder stands the finest lady
That ever your two eyes did see;
She has got rings on every finger
And one of them she has got three.
She has as much gay gold about her clothing
As purchased half of Northumberlee.

"She wants you to send her a slice of bread
And a bottle of your best of wine,
And to not forget that fair young lady
Who did release you from close confine."

Lord Bateman in a passion flew,
He broke his sword in splinters three,
Saying, "I'll care no more, no more for riches
Since this bright youth has crossed the sea."

Then up spoke his young bride's mother,
Which never was known for to speak so free:

"You've made a bride all of my daughter,
What need you further with she?"

"If I've made a bride all of your daughter,
She's none the better nor worse for me;
She came to me with a horse and saddle,
She may go back with a coach and three."

Then he took his lady by the lily-white hand
And led her through from room to room
And changed her name from Susanna Fair
To be the wife of Lord Bateman Esquire.

P

As sung by Mrs. Eleanor Frances Grandey, known to her friends as Gramma Grandey, of Bennington, Vermont, eighty-three years old. Mrs. Grandey's husband was a descendant of Elder Grandey, compiler of the Grandey Manuscript book.

M. Olney, Collector
August 9, 1945

Lord Darker

Lord Darker was a gentleman,
A gentleman of some high degree.
He grew uneasy—most discontented,
Until he took a long voyage at sea.

He sail-ed east, he sail-ed west;
He sail-ed 'round some Turkish shore
Where he was taken and cast in prison
For the space of seven long years or more.

This lord he had one only daughter;
One only daughter, a daughter dear.
She stole the keys of her daddy's prison;
She thought Lord Darker she would set free.

"Have you got houses, have you got lands?
Have you got living of a high degree
That you would give this fair lady
To set you at your liberty?"

"Yes, I've got houses and I've got lands
And I've got living at a high degree
That I would give to you, fair lady,
To set me at my liberty."

She took him to her father's cellar
And drew him the wine so strong
That every drink she drank unto him,
"I wish, Lord Darker, that you were mine!"

Q

As sung by Mrs. Emma Burke of Providence, Rhode Island.
M. Olney, Collector
February 5, 1945

Structure: A B C D (2,2,2,2); Rhythm E; Contour: arc;
Scale: hexatonic

t.c. A-flat.

For mel. rel. see RO 1, 81; SSC, 104; BES, 106.

Lord Baton

Lord Baton was a noble lord,
A noble lord he was of high degree,
And he determined then to go abroad,
His country for to see.

Lord Baton

Tr. M. O.

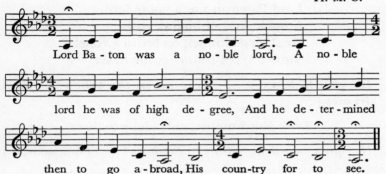

Lord Ba - ton was a no - ble lord, A no - ble
lord he was of high de - gree, And he de - ter - mined
then to go a - broad, His coun - try for to see.

R

*Recorded in Putney, Vermont, from the singing of Mrs.
Herbert Bailey, who remembered this fragment of "Lord
Bakeman" from a play[1] she attended at the Boston Museum
nearly forty-five years earlier.*

H. H. F., Collector
June 3, 1931

Lord Bakeman

Lord Bakeman was a noble lord,
A noble lord he was of high degree,
And he determin-ed to go abroad
Strange countries for to see.

S

*Recorded by George Brown from Mrs. Theodore Sprague
of Readsboro, Vermont, who believes her copy of "Lord
Bateman" (clipped from a newspaper) is like her father's
singing.*

George Brown, Collector
1930

[1] According to Phillips Barry the play was *Rosedale*, or *The Rifle Ball*.

Lord Bateman

Lord Bateman was a noble lord,
A noble lord of high degree.
He shipped himself on board a vessel
Some foreign countries for to see.

[*He goes to Sentipee, a tree grew in the prison, Turkish girl asks,*]

"Doth Northumberland belong to thee?"

[*He splits sword in splinters. Sophia, twenty-one stanzas.*]

T

As sung by Mrs. Lena Bourne Fish of East Jaffrey, New Hampshire. The address was furnished by Mrs. Carl L. Schrader, Chairman of Fine Arts, General Federation of Women's Clubs.

M. Olney, Collector
May 9, 1940 [1]

Structure: A B C^b D (2,2,2,2); Rhythm E; Contour: arc; Scale: hexatonic

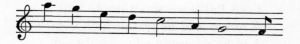

t.c. D.

For mel. rel. see BES, 119; Bruno Nettl, in *Acta Musicologica* (1955), 83, first song.

[1] Mrs. Fish sang the song again the same day with the following variations:

Stanza 3, Line 1: Have you houses and have you lands . . . ?
Line 3: Will you share them with a Turkish princess?
Stanza 4, Line 1: I have houses and I have lands.
Line 3: All of them are yours, my bonnie princess.
Stanza 5, Line 1: She spoke to him kindly words of cheer.
Line 4: She heartily wished that he was her own.
Stanza 6, Line 4: And I will wed no other man.

Lord Bateman

Tr. H. E. F. B.

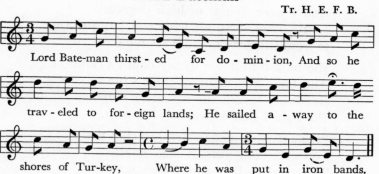

Lord Bate-man thirst-ed for do-min-ion, And so he trav-eled to for-eign lands; He sailed a-way to the shores of Tur-key, Where he was put in iron bands.

Lord Bateman

Lord Bateman thirsted for dominion,
And so he traveled to foreign lands;
He sailed away to the shores of Turkey,
Where he was put in iron bands.

The Turkish king had but one daughter,
A charming maiden and fair to see.
She stole the keys of her daddy's prison
And vowed Lord Bateman she would set free.

"Now have you houses and have you lands,
And have you livings of high degree?
Will you share them with a Turkish maiden
If from this prison she'll set you free?"

Stanza 7, Line 1: Seven long years soon had passed.
            Line 3: Still Bateman waited for his princess.
Stanza 8, Line 2: Asked if Lord Bateman did dwell therein.
Stanza 10, Line 1: Lord Bateman took her by the hand.
            Line 3: She's known no more as Susan Friar.

On July 9, 1941, Mrs. Fish sang the song again with the following additional changes:

Stanza 4, Line 3: All of these are yours, my bonnie princess.
Stanza 7, Line 1: Seven long years had soon passed.

"Yes, I have houses and I have lands,
And I have livings of high degree.
I will share them all with you, my princess,
If from this prison you'll set me free."

She took him down to her daddy's cellar
And bade him drink of their wine so strong,
But every health she drank to Bateman,
She sighed that he was not her own.

"Let's make a pledge and a solemn vow—
For seven long years it shall stand—
That you shall wed no other maiden
Nor I shall wed no other man."

Soon seven long years had gone by
And eight or nine had passed away.
Still Bateman waited for his sweetheart
Although his locks were turning gray.

One day a lady came to his gate,
Asked if Lord Bateman dwelt therein;
"Oh yes," replied the brisk young porter,
"I will call him; please wait within."

"Please ask him if he has forgotten
The Turkish maiden that set him free.
And that my vows are not forgotten,
I am waiting still his bride to be."

He took her by the lily-white hand,
And led her over the marble stone;
She's known no more as a Turkish Princess
For she's now the wife of Lord Bateman.

U

*Contributed by mail by Mrs. Michael Mulcahy of Rutland,
Vermont, as learned in her girlhood in Ireland.*

                              H. H. F., Collector
                              November 15, 1955

Lord Bateman (or Bakeman)

"We made a vow for seven years
And seven days to bind it strong,
That he would wed with no other woman
And she would wed with no other man."

But the seven years are past and over
And the seven days they are at an end
So she packed all her clothing
And said, "Lord Bateman, she would go and see—

When she came to Lord Bateman's palace,
She knocked boldly and rang the bell.
"Who is there? Who is there?" said the proud young waiter.
"Who has knocked so boldly and can't get in?"

"I want to know is this Lord Bateman's palace
Or is his lordship, himself, within."
"Oh yes, oh yes," said the proud young waiter,
"This very day he has his new bride in."

"Go up and ask him for a slice of bread
And a bottle of wine,
If he remembers that fair young lady
That relieved him when close confined."

Lord Bateman got up in such a hurry
That he broke his sword in splinters three.
"Oh yes, oh yes, I . . . .
. . . .

Then up stepped the bride's old mother,
"You wed my daughter". . . .
"Your daughter is none the worse nor the better of me.
"She came here on a horse and pillion
And she can go home with coach and three."

(So the wedding was got ready and everything——)

V

As recited by Mrs. Anna Fiske Hough of Brandon, Vermont.
She learned this from her English mother many years ago.

M. Olney, Collector
May 2, 1940—deteriorated
July 7, 1942—Retake[1]

Lord Bateman

"Is this Lord Bateman's palace?
Is the Lord himself within?

.   .   .   .

.   .   .   .

"Bid him remember three cuts of bread,
Bid him remember the wine so strong;
And ask him if he's forgot the lady
Who set him free from his prison throng (thong?)"

He then rose up from out his chair.
He split the table in pieces three,
Saying, "I'll wage my house and living,
If Susy Fry hasn't crossed the sea.

"Adieu to you, my wedded wife,
For this fair maiden I will see."
Then spoke up the bride's mother,
And she was a lady of high degree.

.   .   .   .

.   .   .   .

"He will forsake our own dear daughter
All for the sake of Susy Fry."

"Your daughter's none the worse for me,
She came here on a horse and saddle;
She shall go home with her coach and three."

[1] The two versions were identical.

W

Recorded in Jamaica, Vermont, from the singing of Fred Ballard, who learned it from his mother, Minervee Hathaway Ballard.

George Brown, Collector
August 27, 1930

Lord Bateman

Lord Bateman into a passion flew
And broke his sword into pieces three,
Saying, "I'll bet my father's money
If Sophia[1] has crossed the sea."

X

Recorded from the singing of George Farnham in Wardsboro, Vermont. Its source is unknown.

George Brown, Collector
August 28, 1930

Lord Bacon

Lord Bacon, he was a worthy knight
About the age of twenty-three
When he was taken and put in prison,
Till he could neither hear nor see.

[1] "Sophia" was pronounced "So-fi."

The Cherry Tree Carol
(Child 54)

Child, II, 1 f., notes the use of this Egyptian legend in the pseudo-Matthew Gospel, Chapter XX, where the tree is a palm. The carol and the legend are known throughout Europe and usually involve cherries, apples, or berries. Irish lore accounts for the low growth of the apple tree by means of this tale, and a form of it was produced annually in the Coventry Mystery Cycle by the Grey Friars.

The song varies in the prophecies that conclude it, although the material is usually founded on Jesus' predictions in the regular Gospels and the angel's words to the shepherds in Luke. Sometimes, the heavenly voices and not the unborn child tell the baffled father of the future, and the mention may be made of Old Christmas Day as the day of Christ's birth. This date will vary from January 5 to 7, depending on which calendar is used.

The text given below follows Child B very closely. This is a version known widely in the chapbooks and on the broadsheets of eighteenth- and nineteenth-century England. The only contributions made to the carol in the convent in Ireland seem to be the reference to Joseph as St. Joseph and to Mary as Blessed Mary. The final portion, opened by a stanza omitted from the Vermont text,

As Joseph was a-walking, he heard the angel sing
"This night there shall be born on earth our heavenly
    king . . ."

is often found as a separate song, "Joseph and the Angel."

See Coffin, 65-67 (American); Dean-Smith, 57 (English); and Greig and Keith, 44-45 (Scottish), for a start on a bibliography. Phillips Barry, *British Ballads from Maine*, 446, found traces of the song.

Printed in Country Songs of Vermont, *48, as learned by Mrs. Ellen M. Sullivan of Springfield, Vermont, in a convent in Ireland about 1860. She said they were taught that Mary was a virgin, that Joseph only came when she needed protection. An earlier and abbreviated singing by Mrs. Sullivan (stanzas 3-7) was recorded in February, 1933, and published in BFSSNE, VI, 14.*

H. H. F., *Collector*
May 26, 1933

Structure: A¹ A² A³ A⁴ (8,8,8,8); Rhythm A; Contour: each phrase descends; Scale: pentatonic with half-tone

t.c. D. Note the small range (major sixth).

For mel. rel. see perhaps Sharp 1, 90; possibly, because of the general simplicity, DV, 565, 13(B).

Cherry Tree Carol

St. Joseph was an old man, an old man was he,
When he met with Blessed Mary on the banks of Galilee.

When Joseph was married and Mary home had brought,
Mary proved with child, and Joseph knew it not.

As Mary and Joseph was walking through a meadow so fair
Where cherries and blossoms were to be seen there,

Blessed Mary

Tr. H. E. F. B.

Then out spoke bless - ed Ma - ry, so soft and so mild, Say - ing, "Pick me a cher - ry, Jo - seph, for I am with child." Then out spoke St. Jo - seph, so keen and so mild, "Let the fa - ther of your ba - by pick cher - ries for thee." Then out spoke our Sav-iour, out of his moth - er's womb, Say - ing, "Bend down, dear cher - ries, let my ma - ma pick some." The high - est branch bend - ed, the low - est branch bowed, Bless - ed Ma - ry picked cher - ries, while her a - pron could hold.

Then out spoke Blessed Mary, so soft [1] and so mild,
Saying, "Pick me a cherry, Joseph, for I am with child."

Then out spoke St. Joseph, so keen and so mild,
"Let the father of your baby pick cherries for thee."

Then out spoke our Saviour, out of His mother's womb,
Saying, "Bend down, dear cherries, let my Mama pick
    thee." [2]

The highest branch bended, the lowest branch bowed.
Blessed Mary picked cherries while her apron could hold.

Our Saviour was not born in a palace or hall
But our Saviour was born in a low ax's[3] stall.

Our Saviour was not dressed in silk or satin so fine
But a piece of fine linen by his own Mama's side.

He neither shall be christened by white wine or red
But with clear spring water as we have been christened.

Then Mary took her baby and set him upon her knee;
"I pray thee now, dear child, tell me how this world it is to
    be."

"Oh, I shall be dead, mother, as the stones in the wall.
Oh, the stones in the street will mourn for me all.

"It will be on a Wednesday my vows shall be paid.
And 'twas on Good Friday, I was crucified.

"On Sunday morning, great sight you will see,
The sun and moon dancing in honor of me."

[1] Sung as "keen" in the *BFSSNE* rendition.
[2] Sung as "some" in the *BFSSNE* rendition.
[3] "ax's": "ox's"

Dives and Lazarus

(Child 56)

Child 56 probably dates from the 1500's when the song of "the Ryche man and poor Lazarus" was licensed with the Registers of the Company of Stationers. The ballad, with its plot both moral and Biblical, became popular in print during the 300 years that followed, appearing on broadsheets, in chapbooks, and in carol collections. One of the most widely circulated volumes to include it was *A Good Christmas Box,* published in Dudley, England, in 1847. Dean-Smith, 63, gives a number of references for texts taken from oral tradition.

The Child form is not known in America, though a similar tale of Dives and Lazarus has been collected fairly frequently in the Southeast. The Flanders fragment, as best one can tell, seems to be of this sort and is unusual only in the fact that it was collected in Vermont. Several other songs, for example, "The Tramp" and "The Little Family," bespeak the popularity of this theme among the American printers. For bibliographical references and discussion of the problems associated with the American "Dives and Lazarus," see Coffin, 67-68, and *The Frank C. Brown Collection* (Durham, 1952———), II, 210-12.

Mrs. Annie Sawyer of Fairfax, Vermont, gave these lines of "Dives and Lazarus."

H. H. F., Collector
September 11, 1956

Dives and Lazarus

[*Lazarus said of Dives,*]

"Even the whelps can eat the crumbs from the master's table."

[*Dives was buried and in Hell. Because he refused Lazarus when he was a rich man, Dives asked for a drop of water*]

"to cool his burning tongue."

[*He looked to Heaven unto Abraham's bosom when he asked for a drop of water, and he asked Abraham to send a message to the earth to his brethren to warn that because they were tightwads as well as he, they should know of his condition. Abraham refused. Mrs. Sawyer said, "I know that, because he said, 'You were warned by the prophets.'"*]

Child Waters

(Child 63)

"Child Waters" is all but extinct in Anglo-American oral tradition. Dean-Smith does not list it at all from England, and besides the present printed text it has been reported only twice from America—a traditional fragment from Arkansas and a full variant of Child B from North Carolina. Child, however, printed eleven versions and considered it to be a ballad with "no superior in English and if not in English perhaps nowhere." He would never have made such a remark had he seen only the *Charms of Melody* "Earl Walter." Here the song has been rewritten as a characteristic melodrama for the eighteenth-nineteenth-century press. Gone is the stark description, the unmoved harshness of the lover, and the direct dramatic close. In its place are trite phrases, sentimentalities of a youth who purposefully submerges his feelings to test his "Griselda," and a death scene (see also Robert Jamieson's *Popular Ballads and Songs from Tradition* [Edinburgh, 1806], I, 113-17) worthy of Little Eva. To read the *Charms of Melody* text in direct comparison to either Child A or B is to see most graphically how the commercial press of 100 to 200 years ago handled the traditional songs.

Coffin, 70, lists the American texts from the collections of Vance Randolph, *Ozark Folk Songs* (Columbia, Mo., 1947-50), I, 69-70, and Frank C. Brown (Durham, N.C., 1952———), II, 65-67, while Greig and Keith, 51-52, prints a

Scottish version. Child, II, 84-85, should be consulted for references to Scandinavian and other analogues.

Copied literatim et punctatim by H. H. F. from a compilation of 400 pages of numbered issues of The Charms of Melody: *or Siren Medley, printed by J. & J. Carrick, Bachelor's Walk, Dublin. The watermark on the title page reads* GREAT NEWTON, *with the date 1818. Copies are available at the Boston Athenaeum; the John Hay Library at Brown University (60 pages, dated 1824, beginning with Volume 1, page 1); and at the Library of Congress.*

H. H. F., Collector
August 1, 1958

Earl Walter

The exquifite and fimple Features of this Tale affords a perfect Model of the ancient Englifh Ballad— We will not attempt to leffen its Merit by our feeble Praife—its numerous affecting Beauties muft prove its beft Recommendation.

EARL Walter frtoked his milk-white fteed,
　His heart with courage beat;
When LO! a damfel—matchlefs fair!
　Fell proftrate at his feet.
"Behold" fhe cried, "a ruin'd maid,
　The victim of thy love,
And let thy Ellen's once-prais'd form,
　Thy tender pity move.

"The dreadful time draws on apace,
　That muft reveal my fhame,
And can earl Walter then confent
　To murder Ellen's fame?

"Ah! wretched infant, doom'd to woe,
  Before thy natal hour,
Difgrace muft be thy portion here,
  Wrong'd Ellen's only dower."

The gallant youth was inly mov'd,
  But coldly thus repli'd,
"The cure that love perhaps difclaims,
  My juftice fhall provide.

"From north to fouth extended wide,
  With fields and paftures fair,
Thofe plains to thee I freely give;
  Beftow them on thy heir."

"By me," fhe cri'd, "more highly priz'd.
  One kifs of that dear mouth,
Than all thy rich and fertile plains,
  Extending north and fouth.

"One glance of thofe deluding eyes
  More rapture can beftow,
Than fhould our monarch quit his throne,
  And that to me forego."

"No more," fair Ellen, "cries the earl,
  I can no longer ftay;
For northward muft I bend my courfe,
  There lies my deftin'd way,"

"With thee, earl Walter, let me go,
  Thy handmaid will I be;
All perils I with joy can brave,
  That much lov'd face to fee."

"Rafh Ellen! doft thou know the terms,
  On which alone thou goeft?
To drop each foft alluring grace,
  Thy fex's pride and boaft,

"Thofe auburn locks to cut away,
  To caft thy woman's weed;
All day to follow as my page,
  All night to 'tend my fteed."

Her auburn locks fhe cut away,
  She caft her woman's weed—
All day fhe follow'd as his page,
  Each night fhe fed his fteed.

At length a rapid ftream they find;
  Which when Earl Walter view'd,
"Thou canft not, Ellen, follow here"—
  He fpoke, and paffed the flood.

But love, than danger ftronger far,
  Her timid heart upbore;
She rufh'd at once amid the waves,
  And reach'd the farther fhore.

But ftill the earl his purpofe kept,
  No pity he confeft,
Tho' ftrong fatigue and anxious care
  The damfel fore opreft.

"Thy languid eyelids, Ellen, raife,
  And view yon princely bow'r;
There pleafure holds his revel reign,
  And marks each paffing hour.

"There dwells a maid more fair than morn,
  Than fummer funs more bright;
That maiden is my plighted love,
  My joy and fole delight."

Sad Ellen mildly anfwer'd thus—
  "May every blifs betide,
And ftill increafing rapture wait
  Earl Walter and his bride."

The princely bower they enter foon,
   And hail the glittering train;
Earl Walter courts each lovely nymph,
   Nor heeds his Ellen's pain.

His fifter with fuperior grace
   Shone far above the reft,
Who, when fhe Ellen's form furvey'd,
   Her wonder thus expreft:

"Ah! whence, my brother, is thy page
   How heavenly fair his face!
What pity that his fize uncouth
   Such beauty fhould difgrace.

"But let the boy on me attend,
   In my apartment wait;
My care fhall footh his gentle mind,
   And mend his prefent ftate."

"Too great for him that honor were,
   A youth of low degree,
Enough diftinguifh'd as my page,
   On foot to follow me."

Now midnight, clofing every eye,
   Left Ellen free to weep,
But with the morn the Earl arofe,
   And broke the bands of fleep.

"Awake! awake! thou flothful page,
   'Tis dawn of breaking day—
Bring forth in hafte my milk-white fteed,
   I muft from hence away."

But ere her lord could be obey'd,
   Uncall'd Lucina came,
And to fad Ellen's other woes,
   She adds a mother's name.

Now burft their way the heart-felt groans,
  Now falls the trickling tear,
'Till thro' the high refounding dome,
  They reach earl Walter's ear.

With eager fteps he fought the place,
  Then made a fearful paufe,
While broken accents breath'd in fighs,
  Reveal the fatal caufe.

"Lie ftill, thou pledge of haplefs love,
  Lie ftill, my infant dear;
I would thy father were a king,
  Thy mother on a bier!"

Enough had now the lover heard,
  He clafps her in his arms,
"Look up my miftrefs, friend, and wife,
  Revive thy drooping charms."

"Thy trial now is fairly paft,
  Thou firft of woman kind:
Thy form, tho' caft in beauty's mould,
  Enfhrines a hero's mind."

"And doft thou know at length my heart?
  Then have I well been tri'd;
I only liv'd to prove my faith:"—
  She grafp'd his hand, and died

Jack, the Jolly Tar

(Laws K 40, possibly related to Child 67)

"Glasgerion," Child 67, is a courtly tragedy of a harper who is invited to the bedroom of the infatuated King's Daughter of Normandy. He tells his boy, Jack, of his tryst and asks Jack to awaken him when it is time to go. Jack instead steals his master's clothes, keeps the rendezvous, and makes churlish, but successful, love to the unsuspecting girl. He then hurries home and arouses his master as though nothing had happened. The harper goes to his lady's chamber where he is asked why he has returned. He denies having been there before; she realizes the truth, and in shame kills herself. The harper goes home, hangs or hacks Jack to death, and goes mad or commits suicide.

The song, in this form, is not known in America. However, both here and in Britain there are a number of songs that use the well-worn motif in which one man takes the place of another to sleep with an unsuspecting girl. Of this sort is "Jack, the Jolly Tar," which is fairly common in New England and which Phillips Barry printed as a "secondary" form of Child 67 in *BFSSNE*, III, 10. "Jack, the Jolly Tar," of course, is not related to "Glasgerion" except in its most general outline. The mood is not gracious, but merry; not tragic, but jestful. The girl's remark on the whole affair, "makes no matter," is quite different from the last words of the Norman lady, "There shall neuer noe churles blood spring within my body."

Child's notes, II, 137, and the article on the "night-visit"

by C. R. Baskerville, *PMLA*, XXXV, 565 f., are helpful
in studying songs like "Jack, the Jolly Tar" and "Glasgerion." Phillips Barry cites Scottish texts and the Scandinavian analogues in *BFSSNE*, III, 11. Laws, *ABBB*, 161,
gives an Anglo-American bibliography.

A

*As sung by George A. Jackson, of Columbia, New Hamp-
shire.*

M. Olney, Collector
July 18, 1941

Structure: A^1 A^2 / B^1 B^2 C D^1 / B^1 E F^c D^2 (1,1,1,1,1,1,1,
1,1,1); Rhythm: generally. B; Contour: undulating; Scale:
major

t.c. C.

Jack the Jolly Tar

As Jack was a-walking through London city,
He had no friends there—no one to pity,
But Jack had heard the people say
That in the streets that he must lay.
Aye and the ding-dang,
Fol-de-diddle laddy-O.

*(For each stanza the third and fourth lines and the refrain
are repeated.)*

He overheard a noble squire
A-talking to his lady there;
Oh, he courted her for many a day
And greeted her both night and day.

As Jack was a-walking through London city,
He had no friends there— no one to pity; But
Jack had heard the people say That in the
streets that he must lay. Aye and the ding-dang, Fol-de-
did-dle lad-dy-O. But Jack had heard the
people say That in the streets that he must lay.
Aye and the ding-dang. Fol-de-did-dle lad-dy-O.

Says he, "Tie a string 'round your little finger
And hang it out the chamber window,
And I'll come up and pull the string
And you'll come down and let me in."

Says Jack, "You can damn my eyes, if I don't venture
To pull that string that hangs out the window."
For Jack comes up and pulls the string,
And she comes down and lets him in.

The squire commenced to curse and swear;
He damned all men and all creation,

Saying: "If your heart is true, then love is true
. . . ."

This fair young maid quickly retired,
Thinking she had her noble squire;
Oh, the squire goes up and pulls the string,
And she comes down and lets him in.

This fair young maid arose quite early,
There laid poor Jack looking so surly.
"What are you here for, you nasty rascal?
You've robbed me of my noble squire.

"Since as it is, 't won't be no better;
We'll join our hands and hearts together."
. . . .
. . . .

B

*Sung by D. H. Raymond of Springfield, Vermont. This is
one of his father's songs.*

H. H. F., Collector
March, 1940

The Esquire and the Maiden

(The Squire was in love with maiden)
"Tie a string on your little finger
And let it down through the bedroom window.
I'll come up and pull the string
And you come down and let me in."
    Fol the dong, fol the day.

"Damned eye," says Jack, "if I don't venture
Pull that string through the bedroom window."
Jack come up and pulled the string.
She come down and let him in.
    Fol the dong, fol the day.

Right to bed they did retire
Thinking she had her heart's desire.
The squire come up to pull the string
And no one there to let him in.
    Fol the ding dong, fol the day.

(She wakened)
"How did you get there, you dirty fellow?"
"I come up and pull the string
And you come down and let me in."
    Fol the ding dong, fol the day.

". . . makes no matter,
We'll join hands and hearts together."
(Jack gets scairt and runs away.)

C

Irish song remembered in fragmentary form by Mrs. G. C. Erskine, of Cheshire, Connecticut.

H. H. F., Collector
October 1, 1939

The Esquire and the Maiden

You step up and pull the string;
I'll step down and let you in.
Whack fol-de-doo-dah,
Diddle liddle luddy aye.

Later, Mrs. Erskine wrote, "Two more lines come to mind."

Up comes Jack in his checkered shirt,
His face and hands all covered with dirt.
Whack fol-de-doo-dah,
Diddle liddle luddy aye.

Young Hunting

(Child 68)

Collecting is sometimes as remarkable in what is not found as in what is found. One would expect an archive as comprehensive as the Flanders archive to include at least one full text of "Young Hunting." That it does not is indicative of the whimsical ways of oral tradition. That the song has been known in New England is evidenced by the tune printed below from Mrs. Parker, by the various confusions concerning the "parrot-endings" on Child 4, "Lady Isabel and the Elf-Knight," as found in New England, and by the fact that Phillips Barry collected it from New Brunswick in 1929 after finding traces of it in Maine. However, it is true the great popularity of the song has been in the South and practically all the citations in Coffin's bibliography and discussion, 71-74, refer to collections from the Appalachian and Southwestern regions. There, its history is quite varied and complicated. See Coffin, 73-74, for a summary. It is no longer found in Britain, where it once had a vigorous Scottish tradition, but it did appear in Delany's *Scotch Song Book* published in New York about 1910.

Young Hunting

Tune only from Mrs. Rosanna J. Parker, Newbury, Vermont. Printed in JAF, *XVIII, 295, by the collector, Phillips Barry.*

Structure: A B C¹ C² (2,2,2,2); Rhythm B; Contour: undulating; Scale: hexatonic

t.c. B-flat.

For mel. rel. see FCB4, 29, No. 18; BES, 122, first half of melody; Sharp 1, 103 (distant).

Young Hunting

Tr. P. B.

Lord Thomas and Fair Annet

(Child 73)

Child prints nine versions of "Lord Thomas and Fair Eleanor" or "The Brown Girl" as the ballad is so frequently called; all but one are Scottish. However, this one, Child D, a seventeenth-century English broadside, seems to be the progenitor of the entire American and modern British stock of the song. Child D variants have been found frequently on both sides of the Atlantic, and this circulation no doubt accounts not only for the fact most informants know or can recognize the ballad, but also for the fact there is little difference in the ballad from one area to another.

Belden, 38, points out some of the major differences between the Scottish tradition and the American versions of the song. The Scottish opening, borrowed from "Fair Margaret and Sweet William" (Child 74), and the remarks exchanged between the women on the brown girl's complexion are both missing in this country, as may be the "rose-briar" cliché, common to Child 74 and Child 75 ("Lord Lovel"). Furthermore, the American hero himself and not his messenger goes to see Eleanor, and he seeks advice from his mother, never other members of the family. As many texts in this country open with a description of Lord Thomas as a "bold forester," the phrase used in the Nafis and Cornish *Forget-me-not Songster,* there is little doubt this popular volume had much to do with the spread and consistency of the ballad throughout the States.

A large bibliography for this song is easy to come by. See

Coffin, 74-76 (American); Dean-Smith, 85, and Belden, 38 (English); and Greig and Keith, 54-57 (Scottish). There is a detailed discussion of verbal variation in Child 73 in *SFQ*, I, No. 4, 25 f., and Reed Smith, *South Carolina Ballads* (Cambridge, Mass., 1928) gives a history of the song. Coffin, 75-76, lists references for play-party variations and for parodies, of which there seem to be a great many.

"Lord Thomas and Fair Annet" has a number of Romance and Germanic analogues. MacEdward Leach, *The Ballad Book* (New York, 1955), 245-46, prints a Danish example. See also Child's remarks, II, 179 f.

The song is in Phillips Barry's *British Ballads from Maine,* 126 f.

The eight tunes for Child 73 seem to belong to three tune families. The largest one consists of five tunes: Kennison, Hayes, MEB, Ballard, and Ashford; within it, MEB and Ballard are closely related, as are Ashford and Hayes. The Edwards and Docherty tunes belong together, while the Moses tune represents a separate category.

A

As sung by Josiah Samuel Kennison of Townsend, Vermont. Mr. Kennison knew this song as a child. He is uncertain as to its source. Published in Vermont Folk-Songs & Ballads, 209

George Brown, Collector
August 23, 1930

Lord Thomas and Fair Eleanor

Lord Thomas, he was a noble lord,
The keeper of king's deer.
Fair Eleanor, she was a lady most bright.
Lord Thomas, he loved her dear.

Structure: A B C^b D C^b D (2,2,2,2,2,2); Rhythm B; Contour: arc; Scale: hexatonic

t.c. G.

For mel. rel. see Sharp 1, 115, 118, 119(D); GCM, 39; FCB4, 36(K); and DV, 569, No. 18(L) (distant).

Lord Thomas and Fair Eleanor

Tr. G. B.

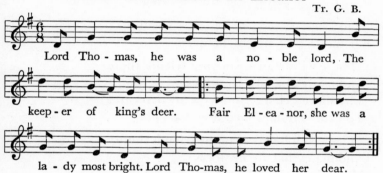

Lord Tho - mas, he was a no - ble lord, The keep - er of king's deer. Fair El - ea - nor, she was a la - dy most bright. Lord Tho - mas, he loved her dear.

(Last half always repeated)

"Advise us both, dear Mother," he says,
"Advise us both as one.
Had I best marry fair Ellen, my dear,
Or bring the Brown Girl home?"

"The Brown Girl she has houses and land;
Fair Eleanor she has none.
Therefore I charge you with my best care
To bring the Brown Girl home."

He call-ed up his merry men all
And dressed them all in white
And every city that he rode through
They took him to be some knight.

He rode till he came to Fair Eleanor's gate.
He knocked aloud on the ring.
There was none as ready as Fair Ellen herself
To rise and let him in.

"Oh, what is the news, Lord Thomas?" she says.
"What news have you brought unto me?"
"I have come to invite you to my wedding."
"Well, that is sad news to me!"

"Advise us both, dear Mother," she says,
"Advise us both as one.
Had I best go to Lord Thomas' wedding
Or had I best stay at home?"

"There will be many of your friends there
And many that 'air' your foes.
Therefore I charge you with my best care,
To Lord Thomas' wedding don't go."

"There will be many of my friends there,
And many that are my foes.
May it bring me life or bring me death,
To Lord Thomas' wedding I'll go."

She call-ed up her merry maids all
And dressed them all in green
And every city that she rode through
They took her to be some queen.

She rode till she came to Lord Thomas' gate.
She knocked aloud on the ring.
There was none so ready as Lord Thomas himself
To arise and let her in.

He took her by her lily-white hand
And led her across the floor
And seated her in a rocking chair
Among the ladies there

"Oh, who is that, Lord Thomas?" she says.
"Methinks she looks wonderful brown.
You might have had as fair a lady
As ever the sun shone on."

"Despise her not," Lord Thomas he says,
"Despise her not unto me.
I have more regard for your little finger
Than I have for her whole body."

The Brown Girl held a knife in her hand,
A knife that was pierce and sharp.
She pierced it into Fair Eleanor's side
And touched her tender heart.

"Oh, what is the matter?" Lord Thomas he says.
"Methinks you look wonderful pale.
The blood that once flowed in your cherry cheeks
Methinks is beginning to fail."

"Oh, 'air' you blind, Lord Thomas?" she says,
"Or can't you very well see?
The blood that once flowed in my cherry cheeks
Is a-trinkling down my knees."

Lord Thomas held a knife in his hand,
A knife that was pierce and sharp.
He cut the head of the Brown Girl off
And kicked it against the wall.

He placed the handle upon the floor
And the point against his heart.
There were never three lovers that ever met
So quick and forever to part.

"Go dig my grave," Lord Thomas he says,
"Go dig it both wide and deep
And bury Fair Eleanor at my side
And the Brown Girl at my feet."

They dug his grave as Lord Thomas had said.
They dug it both wide and deep.
They buried Fair Eleanor at his side
And the Brown Girl at his feet.

B

Sent by George Edwards as sung in his family, of Yorkshire forebears. Mr. Edwards lived in Burlington, Vermont. He wrote, "The last line of each stanza repeats."

H. H. F., Collector
December 13, 1933

Structure: A B C D D (1,1,1,1,1); Rhythm B; Contour: arc; Scale: hexachordal

t.c. E. Note the small range (minor sixth) and the greater length (18/8) of measure 8.

For mel. rel. see MF, 265; DV, 569, No. 18(L).

Lord Thomas

Tr. H. E. F. B.

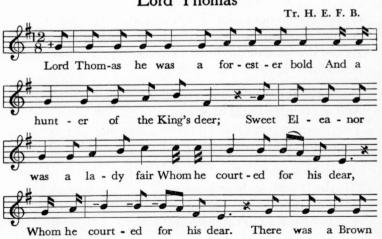

Lord Thom-as he was   a for - est - er bold And a

hunt - er   of   the King's deer;   Sweet El - ea - nor

was   a la - dy   fair Whom he   court - ed   for   his dear,

Whom he   court - ed   for   his dear.   There   was   a Brown

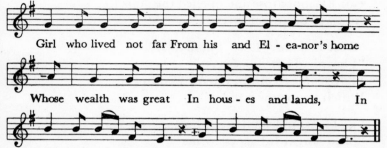

Girl who lived not far From his and El - ea-nor's home

Whose wealth was great In hous - es and lands, In

gold and pre - cious stones, In gold and pre - cious stones.

Lord Thomas

Lord Thomas, he was a forester bold
And a hunter of the King's deer;
Sweet Eleanor was a lady fair
Whom he courted for his dear.

There was a Brown Girl who lived not far
From his and Eleanor's home
Whose wealth was great in houses and lands,
In gold and precious stones.

Long she had sought Lord Thomas' hand
And tried to obtain his love.
She knew that Lord Thomas' mother did
Her actions and aims approve.

"Come read my riddle, dear mother," he said,
"And tell it unto thy son:
Whether Fair Eleanor I shall wed
Or bring the Brown Girl home."

"The Brown Girl she has houses and lands,
Fair Eleanor she has none.
I charge thee, therefore, on my blessing
To bring the Brown Girl home."

Lord Thomas went to Fair Eleanor's home
And knocked loudly at the ring.

Fair Eleanor arose and opened the door
And welcomed her lover in.

"Dear Eleanor," Lord Thomas said,
"I bear bad news to thee.
I have come to bid you to my wedding,
Which tomorrow is to be."

"Bad news indeed, Lord Thomas," she said,
"Most sorrowful news to me
To know that you the Brown Girl will wed
When I your bride should be."

"Come read my riddle, dear mother," she said,
"And tell it unto me,
Whether to Lord Thomas' wedding to go
Or better at home I'll be."

"There's many that are our friends, my dear,
And many that are our foes.
I charge thee, therefore, upon my blessing,
To Lord Thomas' wedding don't go."

"There's many that are our friends, mother dear,
And if thousands were our foes,
Whatever the results of my actions are,
To Lord Thomas' wedding I'll go."

She dressed herself in richest robes
And costliest jewels seen,
And everybody, as she passed by,
Thought her to be a queen.

And when she came to Lord Thomas' door
And softly knocked at the ring,
Lord Thomas himself was waiting there
To let Fair Eleanor in

Lord Thomas took her by the hand
And led her through the room,
And all the guests assembled there
Thought them the bride and groom.

The Brown Girl drew a little penknife;
Its blade was long and sharp;
And between the short ribs and the long
She stabbed Fair Eleanor's heart.

"What is the matter?" Lord Thomas he said,
"Your agony is plain to see."
"Behold, the life blood from my heart
Is trickling down," said she.

Lord Thomas cleft the Brown Girl's head
And flung her against the wall.
The hilt of his sword he placed on the floor
And on its point did fall.

"Oh, dig my grave," Lord Thomas said,
"And dig it both deep and wide;
Place the Brown Girl at my feet,
And Fair Eleanor at my side."

Of all who are caught in Cupid's net
Or pierced by Cupid's dart,
Were ever lovers so lovingly met
And so suddenly did part?

C

*Mrs. Florence Underhill of Bellows Falls, Vermont, with
two sisters, the Misses Young, furnished this song learned
from their father, Edward O. Young (uncle of the former
Dr. Ellis of Brookfield, Vermont).*

H. H. F., Collector
November 2, 1938

Lord Thomas and Fair Eleanor

Lord Thomas he was a bold forester
And a chaser of the king's deer.
Fair Eleanor was a fine woman
And Lord Thomas he loved her dear.

"Come riddle my riddle, dear mother," he said,
"And riddle us both in one,
Whether I shall marry with Fair Eleanor
And let the Brown Girl alone."

"The Brown Girl she has got money.
Fair Eleanor she has none;
Therefore I charge this on my blessing
To bring the Brown Girl home."

And as it befell on a holiday
As many more do beside,
Lord Thomas he went to Fair Eleanor
That should have been his bride.

But when he came to Fair Eleanor's bower
He knock-ed at the ring;
Then who was so ready as Fair Eleanor
To let Lord Thomas in.

"What news, what news, Lord Thomas," she said,
"What news hast thou brought unto me?"
"I am come to bid thee to my wedding,
And that is sad news for thee."

"Oh, God forbid, Lord Thomas," she said,
"That such thing ever should be done.
I thought to have been thy bride myself
And thou to have been the bridegroom."

"Come riddle my riddle, dear mother," she said,
"Come riddle it all in one,

Whether I shall go to Lord Thomas' wedding
Or whether I shall let it alone."

"There's many that are our friends, daughter,
And many that are our foes.
Therefore I charge thee on my blessing
To Lord Thomas' wedding don't go."

"There's many that are our friends, mother;
If a thousand were our foes,
Betide me life, betide me death,
To Lord Thomas' wedding I'll go."

She clothed herself in a gallant attire
And her merry men all was seen
And as she rode through every place
They took her to be some queen.

When she came to Lord Thomas' gate,
She knock-ed at the ring,
And who was so ready as Lord Thomas
To let Fair Eleanor in.

He took her by the lily-white hand
And led her through the hall
And he sat her in the noblest chair
Among the ladies all.

"Is this your bride?" Fair Eleanor said.
"Methinks she looks wondrous brown;
You might have had as fair a woman
As ever trod upon the ground."

"Despise her not," Lord Thomas he said,
"Despise her not unto me.
For better I love her little finger
Than all your whole body."

This Brown Girl had a little penknife
Which was still both keen and sharp

And betwixt the short ribs and the long
She pricked Fair Eleanor to the heart.

"O Christ now save me, Lord Thomas," she said.
"Methinks thou lookest wondrous wan;
Thou used'st to look as good a color
As ever the sun shone on."

"Oh, art thou blind, Lord Thomas," she said,
"Or canst thou not very well see?
Oh, dost thou not see my own heart's blood
Run trickling down my knee?"

"Oh, dig my grave," Lord Thomas replied,
"Dig it both wide and deep
And lay Fair Eleanor by my side
And the Brown Girl at my feet."

Lord Thomas he had a sword by his side
As he walked about the hall;
He cut his bride's head from off her shoulders,
And flung it against the wall.

He set his sword upon the ground
And the point against his heart.
There never was three lovers sure
That sooner did depart.

D

Sung by Mrs. Lily Delorme of Cadyville, New York.
M. Olney, Collector
December 8, 1941

Lord Thomas and Fair Eleanor

Lord Thomas, he was a bold forester
And a chaser of the king's deer.
Fair Eleanor was a fine woman
And Lord Thomas loved her dear.

"Come riddle my riddle, dear mother," he said,
"And riddle it all in one,
If I shall wed with Fair Eleanor
Or bring the Brown Girl home."

"The Brown Girl, she has got money
But Fair Eleanor, she has none;
Therefore, I advise thee, my life blessing,
To bring the Brown Girl home."

He rode till he came to Fair Eleanor's gate
And he knock-ed at the ring.
There was none so ready as Fair Eleanor
To let Lord Thomas in.

"What news, what news, Lord Thomas," she cried,
"What news do you bring unto me?"
"I've come to invite you to my wedding
And that is sad news to thee."

"O God forbid," Fair Eleanor cried,
"That such a thing should happen to me.
I thought to have been a bride myself
And you to have been the bride's groom."

"Come riddle my riddle, dear mother," she said,
"And riddle it all in one,
Whether I should go to Lord Thomas' wedding
Or whether I stay at home."

"There's many that are our friends, daughter,
But many more are our foes.
Therefore, I advise thee by my blessing
To Lord Thomas' wedding don't go."

She dressed herself in gallant attire,
With her merry men all to be seen,
And every town that they rode through,
They took her to be a queen.

And when she came to Lord Thomas' gate,
She knock-ed at the ring.
There was none so ready as Lord Thomas himself
To let Fair Eleanor in.

He took her by the lily-white hand
And led her through the hall
And seated her all in the noblest chair
Around the ladies all.

"Is this your bride, Lord Thomas?" she said,
"Methinks she looks wondrous brown.
You might have had as fair a lady
As ever the sun shone on."

The Brown Girl had a knife in her hand
Which was both keen and sharp.
Betwixt the long ribs and the short
She pierced Fair Eleanor's heart.

"Oh, what is the matter?" Lord Thomas, he cried,
"Methinks you look wondrous wan.
You used to have as fair a color
As ever the sun shone on."

"Oh, art thou blind, Lord Thomas," she said,
"Or canst thou not plainly see?
Canst thou not see that my own heart's blood
Runs trickerling down to my knee?"

Lord Thomas he had a sword in his hand
As he walk-ed through the hall.
He cut his bride's head from her shoulder
And threw it against the wall.

"Go dig my grave," Lord Thomas, he cried,
"And dig it broad and deep,
And lay Fair Eleanor by my side
And the Brown Girl at my feet."

He laid his sword upon the ground,
With the point against his heart,
And there never was three lovers sure
That sooner did depart.

E

Sung by Hanford Hayes of Stacyville, Maine.

M. Olney, Collector
May 6, 1942

Structure: A¹ B A² C (2,2,2,2); Rhythm A; Contour: arc;
Scale: major

t.c. D.

For mel. rel. see Sharp 1, 115, 118, 119(D); SSC, 110, 115;
RO 1, 100.

Lord Thomas and Fair Eleanor

Tr. H. E. F. B.

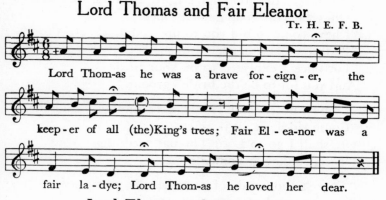

Lord Thomas and Fair Eleanor

Lord Thomas he was a brave foreigner,
The keeper of all (the) King's trees;
Fair Eleanor was a fair ladye;
Lord Thomas, he loved her dear.

"Come riddle, come riddle, dear mother," said he,
"Come riddle it all in one.
Oh, shall I marry Fair Eleanor dear,
Or bring the Brown Girl home?"

"The Brown Girl, she has houses and land;
Fair Eleanor she has none.
Before I'll give you my blessing,
Go bring the Brown Girl home."

He dressed himself in scarlet red,
His merrymens all in green,
And ever-y town that he rode through,
They took him to be some king.

He rode till he came to Fair Eleanor's hall,
He jibbled so loud on the ring.
There was none so ready as Fair Eleanor herself
To rise and let him in.

"Oh, what's the good news, Lord Thomas?" she said,
"Oh, what's the good news for me?"
"I have come to bid you to my wedding."
"Bad news, bad news," cries she,
"For once I expected to be your bride
And you for to be the bride's groom."

"Come riddle, come riddle, dear mother," said she,
"Come riddle it all in one.
Oh, shall I go to Lord Thomas' wedding,
Or shall I stay at home?"

"There's thousands of your friends, you know,
Ten thousand of your foes.
Before I'll give to you my blessing,
To Lord Thomas' wedding don't go!"

She dressed herself in scarlet red,
Her merry maids all in green,

And every town that she rode through,
They took her to be some queen.

She rode till she came to Lord Thomas' hall,
She cabled so loud on the ring.
There was none so ready as Lord Thomas himself
To rise and let her in.

He took her by the lily-white hand,
He led her across the hall.
He placed her on the former seat
'Longside of the ladies all.

"Is this your bride, Lord Thomas?" she said,
"She appears to be wonderful brown.
You might have had as fair a lady
As ever the sun shone on."

"Oh, don't despise her, Fair Eleanor, dear,
Oh, don't despise her to me,
For once I loved your little finger
More than her whole bodie."

"Oh, what's the matter, Fair Eleanor, dear?
You appear to be wonderful pale,
For once your cheeks were cherry-rose red,
But now they are growing pale."

"Oh, what's the matter, Lord Thomas?" she said,
"You appear to be wonderful blind.
Why don't you see my own heart's blood
A-trinkelling down my gown?"

He took the sword out of the sheath.
He walk-ed across the hall.
He cut his own true lover's head off
And dashed it against the wall.

He put the hilt of his sword to the floor,
The point of it to his breast,

Saying, "Was there ever three true lovers met
So quickly put to rest?"

F

*Published in JAF, XVIII, 128. "Recorded February, 1905,
by M. E. B., Irasburg, Vt., from the singing of an aged man
born in Glover, Vt." A note from Phillips Barry indicates
that the singer was Solon Percival.*

Phillips Barry, Collector
February, 1905

Structure: A B C D C D (2,2,2,2,2,2); Rhythm B; Contour:
arc; Scale: pentachordal

t.c. E-flat.

For mel. rel. see Sharp 1, 124(M); SSC, 115; GCM, 39.

Lord Thomas and Fair Annet

Tr. P. B.

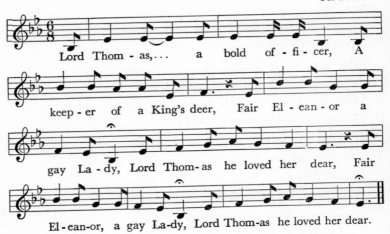

Lord Thom - as,... a bold of - fi - cer, A
keep - er of a King's deer, Fair El - ean - or a
gay La - dy, Lord Thom - as he loved her dear, Fair
El - ean-or, a gay La-dy, Lord Thom-as he loved her dear.

Little Eleanor

Lord Thomas a bold officer,
  A keeper of a King's deer,
Fair Eleanor a gay Lady,
  Lord Thomas he loved her dear.

REFRAIN,—Fair Eleanor a gay Lady,
  Lord Thomas he loved her dear.

"Come riddle us, riddle us, mother," he said,
  "Come riddle us both as one,
Had I better marry Fair Eleanor,
  Or bring the brown girl home?"

"The brown girl, she has houses and lands,
  Fair Eleanor, she has none,
So now I will advise you, as a blessing,
  Go bring the brown girl home!"

He dressed himself in his best attire,
  His clothing all in white,
And every city that he rode through,
  They took him to be some knight.

And when he came to Fair Eleanor's door,
  He knocked so hard on the ring,
There was none so ready as Fair Eleanor,
  To arise and let him in.

"What now, what now?" Fair Eleanor cried,
  "What news do you bring unto me?"
"I have come to invite you to my wedding!"—
  "That's very bad news!" said she.

"Come riddle us, riddle us, mother," she said,
  "Come riddle us both as one

Had I better go to Lord Thomas's wedding,
 Or had I better stay at home?"

"There are few would prove your friends, daughter,
 There are many would prove your foes,
So now I'd advise you as a blessing,
 Lord Thomas's wedding don't go!"

"There's few would prove my friends, mother,
 There's many would prove my foes,
Betide my life, betide my death,
 Lord Thomas's wedding I will go."

She dressed herself in her best attire,
 Her clothing all in green,
And every city that she rode through,
 They took her to be some queen.

And when she came to Lord Thomas's door,
 She knocked so hard on the ring,
There was none so ready as Lord Thomas himself,
 To arise and let her in.

"Is this your bride?" Fair Eleanor cried,
 "To me she looks wondrous wan,
You might have had me, as gay a lady,
 As ever the sun shone on!"

The brown girl, she had a knife in her hand,
 It was both long and sharp,
She placed it against Fair Eleanor's side,
 And pierces it to her heart.

"What ails you, what ails you?" Lord Thomas cried,
 "To me you look wondrous wan,
The blood that was in your cherry red cheeks
 Is all faded away and gone!"

"Oh, where are your eyes?" Fair Eleanor cried,
  "Can't you but skim the seas?
The blood that was in my cherry red cheeks
  Is trickling down my knees!"

Lord Thomas, he had a sword in his hand,
  It was both sharp as an awl,
And with it he cut the brown girl's head off,
  And threw it against the wall.

He laid the sheath down on the ground,
  He put the point through his own heart,
Did you ever see three lovers so soon met,
  That were so soon apart?

G

As sung by Mrs. Lilla Bracey of the Agamenticus section
of York, Maine. Learned from her parents, who were de-
scendants of the early settlers of this part of Maine.
                          M. Olney, Collector
                          September 21, 1947

Lord Thomas and Fair Eleanor

Lord Thomas called his merry men all
And dressed himself in white
And every town that he rode through
They took him to be some knight.

He came unto Fair Eleanor's bower
And knocked upon the ring;
Although so ready as Fair Eleanor
She rose to let him in.

"Oh, what is the matter, Lord Thomas?
Why have you come unto me?"

"I've come to invite you to my wedding."
"Oh, that is sad news!" says she.

Fair Eleanor called her merry men all
And dressed herself in green
And every town that she rode through
They took her to be some queen.

She came unto Lord Thomas' hall
And knocked upon the rim.
Oh, who's so ready as Lord Thomas
He rose to let her in.

"Is this your bride, Lord Thomas?" she cried.
"Methinks she looks wondrous brown.
You might have had as fair a lady
As ever the sun shone on."

"Oh, name her not!" Lord Thomas, he cried,
"Oh, name her not unto me
For better I love your little finger
Than all her whole bodee."

The Brown Girl had a little penknife;
It was both keen and sharp.
Between the short ribs and the long
She pricked Fair Eleanor's heart.

"Oh, what's the matter?" she cried.
"Why, canst thou very well see?
You canst not see my own heart's blood
Go trickerling down my knee?"

He placed his sword upon the floor,
It pointed to his heart;
There never were three lovers, sure,
That sooner did depart.

H

Recorded in Bennington, Vermont, from the singing of Sharon Harrington, as learned from his mother, Mrs. Rebecca Smith Harrington.

George Brown, Collector
September 13, 1930

Lord Thomas

Lord Thomas, he was a bold forester,
A keeper of the King's deer.
Fair Eleanor was a sweet pretty girl.
Lord Thomas he loved her most dear.

"Come, Mother, tell unto us,
Tell us both as one,
Is it best to marry Fair Eleanor
Or bring the Brown Girl home?"

"The Brown Girl, she has houses and land.
Fair Eleanor, she has none
Wherefore, I advise you as my best praises
To bring the Brown Girl home."

So he call-ed up his merry men all
And dressed them all in white,
And every town that he rode through
They took him to be some knight.

And when he came at Fair Eleanor's castle,
He knocks so loud that it ring,
And none was so ready as Fair Eleanor
To arise and let him in.

"Oh, what is the matter?" Fair Eleanor says.
"What news do you bring to me?"
"I've come to invite you to my wedding,
And that is sad news to thee."

"Sad news, sad news," Fair Eleanor says,
"Sad news you bring to me,
For it's once I expected to be your bride—
And that is sad news to me.

"Come, Mother, tell unto us,
Tell us both as one,
Is it best to go to Lord Thomas' wedding,
Or is it best to stay at home?"

"I know there will be many of your daily foes
And many your daily friends,
But therefore I advise you to my best praises
To Lord Thomas' wedding don't go."

"I know there will be many of my daily friends
And many that I know,
But if I knew my life laid at the point of a knife
To Lord Thomas' wedding I'll go."

So she call-ed up her merry maids all
And dressed them all in green,
And every town that she rode through
They took her to be some queen.

And when she came to Lord Thomas' castle
She knocked so loud that it rang.
And none was so ready as Lord Thomas himself
To rise and let her in.

He took her by her lily-white hand
And he led her through the hall.
He seated her at the head of the table
Among the gentry all.

"Is this your bride?" Fair Eleanor said.
"Methinks she looks wonderful brown.

You might a had me, as gay a lady
As ever the sun shone on."

The Brown Girl she had a long penknife,
It being so long, keen, and sharp.
She stabbed Fair Eleanor under the ribs;
She stabbed her to her heart.

"Oh, what is the matter?" Lord Thomas, he says.
"Methinks you look wonderful pale.
Your cherry red cheeks and your ruby lips—
Methinks the color is gone."

"Oh, are you blind?" Fair Eleanor says.
"Or can't you very plain see?
Your own wedded wife has stabbed to my heart
With the blood that's running down by me."

Lord Thomas he had a glittering sword
Which being so long, keen, and sharp,
He cut his own wedded wife's head off
And kicked it against the wall.

[*Mr. Harrington knows he killed himself, too, but could
not remember the lines.*]

Funny, was there ever three lovers that met together
And so suddenly did part.

I

*Sung by John Docherty at the YMCA in Bennington, Ver-
mont, as taught to him by Nellie Hubbard at Barton, Or-
leans County, Vermont. When he was a young boy, recently
come from Scotland, Miss Hubbard, a young Vermont
woman, used to entertain him by singing these old songs.*
                    Alice Brown, Collector
                    July 16, 1930

Structure: A¹ A² A¹ A³ (2,2,2,2); Rhythm A; Contour: each
line an arc; Scale: hexatonic

t.c. **G.**

For mel. rel. see MF, 265; FCB4, 30, No. 19(A).

Lord Thomas and Fair Eleanor
Tr. A. B.

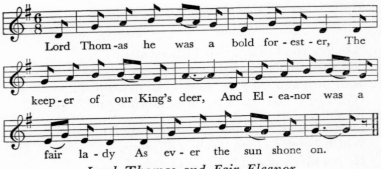

Lord Thomas and Fair Eleanor

Lord Thomas he was a bold forester,
The keeper of our King's deer;
And Eleanor was a fair lady.
Lord Thomas he loved her dear.[1]

"Come riddle, come riddle, kind mother," he said;
"Come riddle us both as one
Whether shall I marry the Fair Eleanor
Or bring the Brown Girl home."

"The Brown Girl she has got money and lands;
Fair Eleanor she has got none.
Therefore I command you as my blessing
To bring the Brown Girl home."

He dressed himself and he decked himself
And his merry men all in white

[1] Note that this line differs as given with tune.

And every town that he passed through
They took him to be some knight.

When he arrived at Fair Eleanor's bower
How loudly his knock did ring,
And none more ready than Eleanor herself
To arrive and let him in.

"What is the news, Lord Thomas," she said,
"What news do you bring unto me?"
"I have come to invite you to my wedding."
"That's very bad news," said she.

She dressed herself and she decked herself
And her merry maidens all in green
And every town that she went through
They took her to be some queen.

And when she arrived at Lord Thomas' castle
How loudly her knock did ring,
And none were more ready than Sir Thomas himself,
To arise and let her in.

"Is this your bride, Lord Thomas?" she said.
"She seems so wonderfully brown.
You might have as fair a lady
As ever the sun shone on."

The Brown Girl held in her hand a knife;
It was both keen and sharp.
She stabbed Fair Eleanor twix the ribs
And pierced her tender heart.

"What is the matter?" Lord Thomas he said.
"You seem to look wonderful wan;
You used to be as fair a lady
As e'er the sun shone on."

"Oh, are you blind, Lord Thomas?" she said.
"Or cannot you very well see

That my heart's blood this very moment
Comes trickling down to my knee?"

He took the Brown Girl by the hand
And led her through the hall
And there he cut off his own bride's head
And threw it against the wall.

J

As sung by Jonathan Moses of Orford, New Hampshire.
M. Olney, Collector
July 10, 1943

Structure: A B A B (2,2,2,2); Rhythm A; Contour: each line an arc; Scale: pentachordal

t.c. B-flat. Note the large range and the large melodic intervals

For mel. rel. see Sharp 1, 127(T); and perhaps GCM, 37.

The Brown Girl

Tr. M. O.

1. "Had I bet-ter go to Lord Thom-as'
wed-ding, Or had I bet-ter tar-ry at
home?" "Oh I would ad-vise it by
my bless-ing, Lord Thom-as' wed-ding—don't go."

2. She dress - ed up her wait - ing maids all; She

dressed them all up in green, And

ev - 'ry town that she rode through, They

took her to be some queen, And

ev - 'ry town that she rode through; They

took her to be some queen.

The Brown Girl

"Had I better go to Lord Thomas' wedding,
Or had I better tarry at home?"
"Oh, I would advise it by my blessing,
Lord Thomas' wedding—don't go!"
   (*Last two lines of each stanza repeated*)

She dress-ed up her waiting maids all;
She dressed them all up in green,
And ev'ry town that she rode through,

They took her to be some queen.
And ev'ry town that she rode through,
They took her to be some queen.

She rode till she came to Lord Thomas' door,
And knock so loud at the[1] ring;
And none were so ready as Lord Thomas
To 'rise and to let her in.
And none were so ready as Lord Thomas
For to arise and let her in.

He took her by her lily-white;
He led her through the hall;
He placed her at the head of his own table
Among the gentries all.

"Is that your bride?" Fair Eleanor said.
"I think she looks wonderful brown;
For you might have had as fair a lady
As ever the sun shone on!"

She drew a penknife from her sleeve;
She pierced through their heart,
Saying, "There never were three lovers that met
Could any sooner part!"

He took the Brown girl by the hand;
He marched her through the hall;
He took her brown head off at one stroke
And kicked it against the wall.

He placed the handle to the floor,
The[1] point right through his heart,
Saying, "There never was three lovers that met
Could any sooner part!"

[1] "the" pronounced "ther

K

Recorded in Jamaica, Vermont, from the singing of Fred Ballard, 72.

George Brown, Collector
August 27, 1930

Structure: A B C D (2,2,2,2); Rhythm A; Contour: arc;
Scale: hexatonic

t.c. G.

For mel. rel. see Sharp 1, 124(M); SSC, 115; DV, 568, No. 18(B).

Lord Thomas

Tr. G. B.

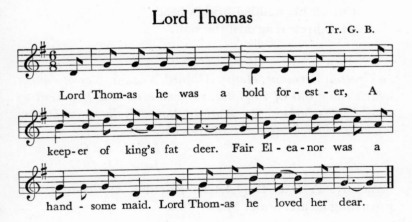

Lord Thomas he was a bold forester, A keeper of king's fat deer. Fair El-ea-nor was a hand-some maid. Lord Thomas he loved her dear.

Lord Thomas

Lord Thomas he was a bold forester,
A keeper of king's fat deer.
Fair Eleanor was a handsome maid.
Lord Thomas he loved her dear.

"O, mother, dear mother," Lord Thomas said,
"Come tell us both as one.
Had I better marry Fair Eleanor
Or bring the Brown Girl home?"

"The Brown Girl, she's got house and land.
Fair Eleanor, she has none.
Therefore I advise you with my blessing
Go bring the Brown Girl home."

. . . .

The Brown Girl had a knife in her hand,
It being both small and sharp.
She stabbed Fair Eleanor in her side
Which touched her tender heart.

Lord Thomas drew his sword and—

Cut off his wedded bride's head
And threw it against the wall.

L

*In Groton, Vermont, Henry Ashford, a call-fiddler of dances
which came out of England, remembered this fragment as
sung by his father. Mr. Ashford formerly lived in Derby,
New Brunswick, near the Miramichi.*

*H. H. F., Collector
June 22, 1937*

Structure: A B C D (4,4,4,4); Rhythm A; Contour: approaching an arc; Scale: Mixolydian

t.c. D.

For mel. rel. see Sharp 1, 115, 118, 119(D); DV, 570, No. 18(S).

Lord Thomas

Tr. M. O.

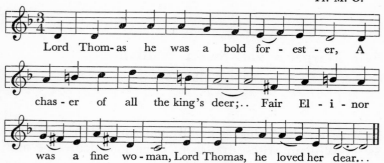

Lord Thom-as he was a bold for - est - er, A
chas - er of all the king's deer;.. Fair El - i - nor
was a fine wo - man, Lord Thomas, he loved her dear...

Lord Thomas

Lord Thomas, he was a bold forester,
A chaser of all the king's deer;
Fair Elinor was a fine woman.
Lord Thomas, he loved her dear.

"Come riddle my riddle, dear mother," he said,
"And come riddle us both into one,
Whether I should marry Fair Elinor
Or bring the Brown Girl home."

"The Brown Girl, she has money and lands,
And Fair Elinor, she has none,
And before I charge you with my blessing,
Bring the Brown Girl home."

. . . .

"Dig my grave," Lord Thomas, he said,
"And dig it both wide and deep;
Lay Fair Elinor at my side
And the Brown Girl at my feet."

Fair Margaret and Sweet William
(Child 74)

In America this ballad generally tells the following story: Sweet William arises, dresses in blue, and denies he and Lady Margaret are in love. He states, moreover, that she will see his bride the next day. Margaret, who watches William's wedding procession pass her window, throws down her comb, leaves the room, and is never more seen alive. That night William is awakened to see Margaret's ghost at the foot of his bridal bed. The ghost asks him how he likes his bride, and he replies he loves the person at the foot of his bed far better. Later he goes to see Margaret, after informing his wife of the vision. Her family shows him the body, and he kisses the "cold, clay lips" before dying. This narrative, while substantially like those in Child, differs consistently in a number of details. The opening scene on the hillside of Child A is dropped, and there is the development of a scene in which William asks his bride's permission to go see Margaret. A brief summary of these American changes is given in Coffin, 77-78. However, the "rose-briar" ending, which sometimes takes up fifty per cent of the singer's time, is ever-present here as in Britain, as is the material so frequently borrowed by this song from Child 73, "Lord Thomas and Fair Annet," and Child 75, "Lord Lovel."

Few ballads have been more popular with Anglo-American folk singers than "Fair Margaret and Sweet William." This is because of its inclusion in many of the early songsters

122

and on a number of broadsheets. Even though we have no extant text from earlier than the eighteenth century, we know its tradition in print goes back to about 1600, for it is quoted in Act II, scene 8, and again in Act III, scene 5, of Beaumont and Fletcher's *The Knight of the Burning Pestle*.

The Flanders A text is similar to Child B, as the bride and not William has the dream. Flanders B and the H fragment are standard American texts in which William dresses in blue at the start. The other Flanders material, C-G and I, is not unusual and one text is quite like the other, although all leave out the dressing in blue. In most of them, see D and E, for example, it is difficult to follow the story. In fact, with the omission of detail, the texts, excepting F perhaps, are actually well on the way to a completely new plot that includes no ghostly visitation. Recent collecting, however, has shown this development to be quite common to the tradition of the song.

For a start on a bibliography, see Coffin, 76-78 (American); Dean-Smith, 65, and Belden, 48 (English); and Child's remarks, II, 74 f. Barry, *British Ballads from Maine*, 134 f., includes the song.

The five tunes given here are not closely related. Possibly all are independent, or they may fall into the following three groups: 1) Davis and Haskins; 2) Erskine and Hartwell; and 3) Ashford. Definitely close relatives have also been hard to find in other collections.

A

*Asa Davis of Milton, Vermont, sang this song as learned
from his father, Joel Davis of Duxbury, Vermont. Printed
in* Ballads Migrant in New England, *83.*[1]

H. H. F., Collector
June 23, 1939
Re-take May 8, 1943

Structure: A B C D (2,2,2,2); Rhythm D; Contour: undulating; Scale: hexatonic

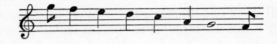

t.c. C.

For mel. rel. see perhaps Sharp 1, 145(O).

King William and Fair Margaret

Tr. H. E. F. B.

La - dy Mar - garet was go - ing to the

high bow - er All for to comb her hair. She

saw King Wil - liams and his bride A - go - ing to

church for prayer. She threw down her i - vor - y comb; Threw

back her yel - low hair: She threw her - self from the

---

[1] The 1939 singing omitted stanzas 12 and 16.

high bow - er And swore she would lie there. La - dy

Mar - garet died in the mid - dle of the night When

all the rest were (a-) sleep. Her spir - it left her

fair bod - ee And stood at Wil - liams' feet. "Oh,

how do you like your bed", said she, "And

how do you like your sheets And how do you like that

fair la - dee That in your arms doth sleep?"

"Well do I like my bed," said he, "And well do I

like my sheets But bet - ter do I like that

fair la - dee That stands at my bed's feet". King

Wil - liam's bride a - woke. "I had a woe - ful

dream", said she; "I hope it nev-er'll prove true— I

dreamt our cel - lar was filled with white wine; La - dy

Mar - ga - ret died for you." "That is a woe - ful

dream", said she; "I hope it nev-er'll prove true, But

I'll go up to the high bow - er A -

mem - ber days a - new." King Wil - liams went to the

high bow - er; He knocked so loud as to ring.

There was none so read - y as her own broth - er was

To a - rise and let him in. "Oh, is she in the

kitch - en," said he, "Or is she in the hall,

Or is she in the long cham - ber— The

up - per room of all?" "She is not in the

kitch- en," said she, "Nor is she in the hall. But

she] is in the long cham - ber dead With her

face turned to the wall." He fold - ed down the

milk-white sheets That were spread up o - ver her head And

there he saw both black and yel - low Where it

used to be white and red. Twice he kissed her

cheek, he said, And twice he kissed her chin, And

twice he kissed those clay-cold lips Where there was no

breath with-in.   La-dy Mar-gar-et died in the

mid-dle of the night. Sweet Wil-liams he died on the

mor-row.   La-dy Mar-'gret died for pure good love;

Sweet Wil-liams he died for sor-row.   La-dy

Mar-'gret was bur-ied in the high church yard; Sweet

Wil-liams was bur-ied there be-side her.   And

out of La-dy Mar-gar-et's breast grew a rose And

out of Sweet Wil-liam's a briar. They grew till they

grew to the high church top Where they could not

grow an - y high - er. There they tied them-selves in a
true lov - er's knot and they died a - way to -
geth - er. Come, all young men and maid-ens,
See this rose and the bri - ar meet. 'Tis e -
nough to break the hard - est of hearts
And the dri - est of eyes for to weep.

King William and Fair Margaret

Lady Margaret was going to the high bow-er
All for to comb her hair.
She saw King Williams and his bride
A-going to church for prayer.

She threw down her ivory comb;
Threw back her yellow hair;
She threw herself from the high bow-er
And swore she would lie there.

Lady Margaret died in the middle of the night
When all the rest were asleep.
Her spirit left her fair bodee
And stood at Williams' feet.

"Oh, how do you like your bed," said she,
"And how do you like your sheets
And how do you like that fair la-dee
That in your arms doth sleep?"

"Well do I like my bed," said he,
"And well do I like my sheets
But better do I like that fair la-dee
That stands at my bed's feet."

King Williams' bride awoke.

"I had a woeful dream," said she;
"I hope it never'll prove true—
I dreamt our cellar was filled with white wine;
Lady Margaret died for you."

"That is a woeful dream," said she;
"I hope it never'll prove true,
But I'll go up to the high bower
A-member days anew."

King Williams went to the high bower;
He knocked so loud as to ring.
There was nōne so ready as her own brother was
To arise and let him in.

"Oh, is she in the kitchen," said he,
"Or is she in the hall,
Or is she in the long chamber—
The upper room of all?"

"She is not in the kitchen," said she,
"Nor is she in the hall.
But she is in the long chamber dead
With her face turned to the wall."

He folded down the milk-white sheets
That were spread up over her head

And there he saw both black and yellow
Where it used to be white and red.

Twice he kissed her cheek, he said,
And twice he kissed her chin,
And twice he kissed those clay-cold lips
Where there was no breath within.

Lady Margaret died in the middle of the night.
Sweet Williams he died on the morrow.
Lady Margaret died for pure good love;
Sweet Williams he died for sorrow.

Lady Margaret was buried in the high church yard;
Sweet Williams was buried there beside her.
And out of Lady Margaret's breast grew a rose
And out of Sweet Williams' a briar.

They grew 'til they grew to the high church top
Where they could not grow any higher.
There they tied themselves in a true lover's knot
And they died away together.

Come, all young men and maidens,
See this rose and the briar meet.
'Tis enough to break the hardest of hearts
And the driest of eyes for to weep. [*Last three words spoken*]

B

*About 1917-18 this was sung by Franklin Smith to his son,
Herbert Wilson Smith, at the son's mining camp near So-
corro, New Mexico. In parentheses his father wrote different ways he remembered it. His son thinks his father learned
it from "Grandma" Joy where he boarded in 1884 when
attending Fayette Normal School, Fayette, Ohio. She was
a sprightly lady who lived to be 101 years old. Both men
liked this song and the father was likely to sing this and*

other songs when they were together, as they often were
in New England. Copied literatim et punctatim.

H. H. F., *Collector*
July 24, 1957

Sweet William and Lady Margaret

Sweet William rose on a May morn bright
And dressed himself in blue
Pray tell me of this undying love
That's between Lady Margaret and you

I know no wrong of Lady Margaret
And she knows no wrong of me.
Tomorrow's morn by eight oclock
Lady Margaret's my bride to be.

Lady Margaret stood in her window high
A combing her golden hair
In the church she did espy
Sweet William and his bride pass there

She then threw down her ivory comb
She tossed back her golden hair
That window high she fell back from
And never more was she seen there

When that day was done and night had come
And good men were asleep
Sweet William saw like in a dream
Lady Margaret stood (stand) at his bed feet

How like you now your bed asked she?
And how like you now your sheet
And how like you now your wedded wife
There on your arm asleep
(That lies in your arms asleep)

Fair well (very well) in truth I like my bed
Fair well I like my sheet
But better than both that fair lady
(Far Better I like that fair lady)
A standing at my bed's feet

When that night was done and day was come
(The long night done then day did come)
All good men were awake
(Then good men did awake)
Sweet William's thoughts did trouble him
Of Lady Margaret standing at his bed's feet
(Of Lady Margaret's words at his bed's feet)

Sweet William rose on this May morn
Once more he dressed in blue
He stepped up in his stirrup high
And rode off through the early dew

He rode up to Lady Margaret's hall
He tingered (tingled) at the bell knocker.
Who then arose to let him in?
T'was Lady Margarets seventh brother.

Where is Lady Margaret fair?
Is she in her chamber hall?
Or does she comb her yellow hair
Behind her window wall?

She lies in her chamber hall
She lies in her bed sheet
Her cold face is against the wall
And candles burn at her bed feet

Up spoke Sweet William at this sad time
"Unfold from her face that white bed sheet
That I may kiss those cold cold lips
That so often have kissed mine

"Stand back, go home" her brothers spake
Go back now to your wedded wife
Let our fair sister lie alone
Where for her love she lost her life

Lady Margaret died on one (that) fair day.
Sweet William on the morrow.
Lady Margaret died for her true love
Sweet William died of sorrow.

They laid Lady Margaret in that churchyard
They laid Sweet William near by her
From her grave grew a red red rose
From his a green green brier.

They grew up to the church wall top
Till they could grow no higher
They turned and twined in a lover's knot
Red Rose and Green Brier
(The Rosy and the Brier)

C

As sung by Miss Winifred Haskins of Savoy, Massachusetts.
This ballad was taught to her when she was a small child
by her father's eldest sister, Eliza Ann (Haskins) Maynard.
Printed in Ballads Migrant in New England, *80.*

H. H. F., *Collector*
August 5, 1934

Structure: A^1 A^2 B^a C (2,2,2,2); Rhythm D; Contour: arc;
Scale: hexatonic

t.c. E.

For mel. rel. see Sharp 1, 132.

Prince William and Lady Margaret

Tr. M. O.

Prince Wil - liam   he   court - ed   La - dy
Mar - g'ret   fair,   De - ter - mined to make her his
wife;   They   dif - fered   a - bout   a
small   tri - fle,   Which caused   them both   their   life.

14

Prince William and Lady Margaret

Prince William he courted Lady Marg'ret fair,
Determined to make her his wife;
They differed about a small trifle,
Which caused them both their life.

Prince William he a-hunting went—
A-hunting for a deer—
But who should he meet but Margaret sweet
A-walking to take the air.

He said that "I'm no man for you,
And you're no girl for me—
Before three merry, merry more days,
My wedding you shall see."

She said, "If I'm no girl for you
And you're no man for me,
Before three merry, merry more days
My funeral you shall see."

Lady Margaret she sat at her bowery window
A-combing out her hair;
She saw Prince William and his bride pass by—
To church they did repair.

Lady Margaret she threw down her ivory comb
And toss-ed back her hair.
She threw herself out of her bowery window
And was seen alive no more.

Prince William he dream-ed a troublesome dream,
His dream it was not good;
He dreamed that his bowery was on fire
And Margaret lay covered with blood.

Prince William arose and away he went
And knock-ed at the ring;
There was none so ready as Margaret's brother
To arise and let him in.

It was "How do you do?" and "How do you do?"
And "How does fair Margaret do?"
"Fair Margaret is dead, lying on her cold bed—
And she died for the love of you!"

"Go roll away the winding sheet
That I may view the dead,
That I may kiss those cold pale lips
That once were cherry red.

"I'll kiss those cold pale lips again
Though they never will smile on me;
I made a vow by the powers above
I'd marry none but she."

Lady Margaret she died on that same day—
Prince William he died on the morrow;
Lady Margaret she died of pure love alone—
Prince William he died of sorrow.

Lady Margaret was buried by the salt sea side—
Prince William he was buried by her;
And out of Lady Margaret's grave sprung a red rose
And out of Prince William's a briar.

They grew so high; they grew so tall;
They reached the mountain top;
They grew so high and they grew so tall,
They tied in a true lover's knot.

Now all young people as you pass by
And see where these two lovers do sleep,
Remember that pure love is better than gold,
Though many die for its sake.

D

*Sung by Miss Maude Horton in Poultney, Vermont, as
known to her mother, of English forebears. A native of Mt.
Holly, Vermont, she was born Ellen French, in 1836. This
tune seems a variant of "Johnny Scot" as sung by Jonathan
Moses, of Orford, New Hampshire. Sung from her written
lines, of which this is a copy.*

H. H. F., Collector
April 22, 1946

King William and Lady Margaret

King William was a hunting man
A hunting of the deer,
  (He courted such a girl as
Lady Margaret was;   } Repeat
All on a fine summer year.)

Lady Margaret sat in a high window,
A combing of her hair;
(And who did she see but King William
And his bride a-
Going to church together) (Repeat)

Down she threw her ivory comb
And "tossted" back her hair,
(She threw herself out the bar window
And never saw light any more.)

King William dreamed a troublesome dream,
His dream it was not good,
(He dreamed that his bower house was all on fire;
And his bride's chamber full of blood.)

King William rose, put on his clothes
And told it to his dear,
(I will go and see how Lady Margaret is;
By the leave of you, my dear.)

Up he goes and down he goes,
And knocks all aloud at the ring,
(There was no one so ready as
Lady Margaret's brother to arise and let him in.)

Is she in the parlor, he says,
Or is she in the hall,
(Or is she in the long chamber,
The uppermost room of all.)

She is not in the parlor, he says,
Nor is she in the tee,
(But she is dead in the long chamber
Who died for the love of thee.)

He turned down the milkwhite sheet
And viewed her body dead,

(Methinks thou are a paler one,
I left you cherry red.)

I will kiss your clay cold lips,
Although you can't kiss mine,
(And I will make a solemn vow
And never kiss lips after thine.)

Lady Margaret died on yesterday,
King William died on the morrow.
(Lady Margaret died for pure true love,
King William died of sorrow.)

Lady Margaret was buried in the high church yard,
King William was buried beside her;
(And out of her grave sprung a red rose
And out of his a briar.)

The red rose and the briar grew,
They grew to the mountain top
(The red rose and the briar met
And tied in a lover's knot.)

The red rose and the briar grew,
They grew to the top of the spire,
(The red rose and the briar met
And died away together.)

Come all ye people that pass by
And view these two bodies asleep.
(It will cause the hardest heart to ache,
And the driest eye to weep.)

E

*Sung by Charles A. Greene of Woodstock, Vermont, as
learned when a young man from a man who lived near
Charlotte, Vermont. Mr. Greene was unable to record
because he was a sick man.*

M. Olney, Collector
May 20, 1941

King William and Lady Margaret

King William was a hunting man,
A-hunting up his deer;
He courted such a gal as Lady Margaret was,
All on a summer's day.

Says he, "I'm not the man for you,
Nor you the girl for me.
Before six months has passed and gone,
My wedding you will see."

"If I am not the girl for you
Nor you're the man for me,
Before six months has passed and gone
My burial you will see."

One day King William and his bride
Were going to church together,
And they were walking side by side
Conversing of the weather.

Lady Margaret stood at her bower window
A-combing out her hair,
When she saw King William and his bride
A-going to church together.

She threw down her ivory comb,
And tossing back her hair,
She threw herself from her high bower window
And never saw light any more.

King William dreamt a curious dream,
And that it was not good;
He dreamt the bower was all on fire,
And Lady Margaret's room was full of blood.

Lady Margaret, she died on that same day;
King William, he died on the morrow.

Lady Margaret, she died of love alone;
King William, he died of sorrow.

Out of Lady Margaret's grave grew a red, red rose;
Out of King William's grew a briar;
There they 'twined themselves in a true lover's knot
And both died there together.

F

*Recorded from the singing of Josiah Kennison of Towns-
hend, Vermont. Printed in* Vermont Folk-Songs & Ballads,
213.

H. H. F., *Collector*
October 24, 1930

Lady Margaret and Sweet William

"If you're no woman for me
And I'm no man for you,
Before three merry, merry months are passed
My wedding you shall see."

"If you're no man for me,
And I'm no woman for you,
Before three merry, merry months are passed
My burial you shall see."

As Lady Margaret was sitting in her high chamber window
Combing back her yellow golden hair,
She saw Sweet William with his new bride
Walking to the church together.

She hove the comb in high vo-ree[1]
And tossed back her yellow golden hair.
She flung herself out of the high chamber window
Saying, "I will never go there!"

.   .   .   .

[1] "fury"?

"How do you like your bed,
And how do you like your sheet,
And how do you like that fair lady
That lies in your arms asleep?"

"Very well do I like my bed,
Very well do I like my sheet,
But the best of it all is that fair lady
That stands at my bed feet."

Lady Margaret died in the dead of night.
Sweet William died on the morrow.
Lady Margaret was buried in the high churchyard.
Sweet William was buried there by her.

There sprang a rose from Lady Margaret's grave
And from Sweet William's a briar;
They grew till they grew to the high tree tall

.   .   .   .

They tied themselves in a true love's knot,
And they both died together.

G

*Mrs. G. C. Erskine of Chesire, Connecticut, sang this song
as learned from her neighbor, Mrs. Harriman of Norway,
Maine.*

*H. H. F., Collector
October 1, 1939*

Structure: A B C D (2,2,2,2); Rhythm D; Contour: arc;
Scale: major

t.c. C. Note the triadic movement.

For mel. rel. see RO 1, 109 (distant); EO, 34.

King William and Lady Margaret

Re-take by M. O., Tr. H. E. F. B.

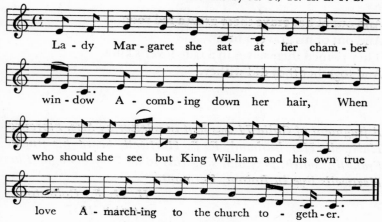

La - dy Mar - garet she sat at her cham - ber win - dow A - comb - ing down her hair, When who should she see but King Wil-liam and his own true love A - march-ing to the church to - geth - er.

King William and Lady Margaret

King William he was a hunting man:
He hunted for his deer.
He courted such a lady as Lady Margaret was
All on one summer's year.[1]

Lady Margaret she sat at her chamber window
A-combing down her hair
When who should she see but King William and his own
true love
A-walking to the church together.

She threw down her ivory comb,
And putting back her hair
She threw herself out of the chamber window
Where never saw light any more.

King William he died as it were today;
Lady Margaret she died on the morrow;

[1] Mrs. Erskine sang "A long, long summer's year" when she repeated the song for Miss Olney on May 9, 1945. The rest of her wording was almost identical.

Lady Margaret she died of pure, pure love.
King William he died of sorrow.

And out of her grave there grew a red rose;
And out of his grave, a briar.
They twined themselves in a true lover's knot
And together they did wither.

H

A fragment of Child 74 was sent in a letter by Mrs. Florence
Hartwell. Her husband, F. E. Hartwell, heard his uncle,
Franklin Smith, play and sing this some 75 years ago. The
Hartwells live in Bolton, Vermont.

H. H. F., *Collector*
April 8, 1957

Structure: A¹ B¹ A² B² (2,2,3,2)—for the first stanza only;
Rhythm D; Contour: undulating; Scale: hexatonic

t.c. F.

For mel. rel. see DV, 572, No. 19(K) (distant); "Geordie,"
from Indiana, L.C. record 1743 A 3.

Lady Margaret and Sweet William

Sweet William arose one very merry morn
And dressed himself in blue,
Saying, "Can you tell me of that long-loving love
That's between Lady Margaret and me?"

[. . . *a number of stanzas . . . and finally wound up with*
a tragic ending where they were buried in the old church
yard, and . . .]

Lady Margaret and Sweet William

Tr. H. E. F. B.

Sweet Wil - liam a - rose one ver - y mer - ry

morn And dressed him - self in blue, Say -

ing, "Can you tell me of that long - lov - ing love

that's be - tween La - dy Mar-garet and me?"..........

Out of her grave grew a sweet climb-ing rose And

out of his grew (a) briar. They grew and they grew to the

church stee - ple top, Till they could not grow an - y

high - er, And there they en - twined in a

true lov - er's knot, The ros - y and the briar.

Out of her grave grew a sweet climbing rose
And out of his grew a briar.

They grew and they grew to the church steeple top
Till they could not grow any higher,

And there they entwined in a true lover's knot,
The rosy and the briar.

I

*Henry Ashford of Groton, Vermont, who lived his early
years in New Brunswick, remembered these few lines as he
heard his father sing them. Because he felt shy about singing,
he played the tune on his fiddle.*

                                H. H. F., *Collector*
                                June 22, 1937

Structure: A B C D (2,2,2,2); Rhythm E but divergent;
Contour: undulating; Scale: major

t.c. F.

Fair Margaret and Sweet William

Tr. M. O.

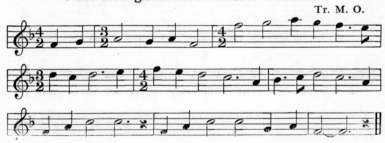

Fair Margaret and Sweet William

" 'Tis now I will go to my chambers above
And I'll never come down any more."

. . . .

Sweet William he died on his wedding day.
Fair Margaret she died on the morrow.

Out of Fair Margaret's breast there growed a red rose
And out of Sweet William there growed a briar.

And they growed up to the high church top
Where they could not grow no higher.
Then they knotted in a true lover's knot,
Both the red rose and the briar.

Lord Lovel

(Child 75)

Phillips Barry in *British Ballads from Maine*, 145-47, gives a good history of this song, telling of its popularity among the nineteenth-century printers and the many uses it served for political parody and music hall gaiety. The American versions which are known wherever ballads are sung almost all stem from the same tradition as Child H, an 1846 London broadside. American printers reproduced texts from this tradition throughout the period between the Mexican and Civil Wars. The Flanders versions are in no way exceptional and are much what one would expect to find. As with texts from other areas, the original name of the church, St. Pancras (see E), has undergone radical modification, but all in all proximity to print has held variation to a minimum.

The tune to "Lord Lovel" is also consistent. In *South Carolina Ballads* (Cambridge, Mass., 1928), 121, Reed Smith comments that "the difference between reading [Lord Lovel] as a poem and singing it is the difference between tragedy and comedy." The use of a tune that is too light for the story no doubt accounts for the fact that parodies have turned up in Maine, Vermont, Virginia, West Virginia, and Missouri, among other places, in this country (see Coffin, 79, for a bibliography) and in Scotland (see Greig and Keith, 57) abroad.

Bibliographical references can be had in Coffin, 78-79

(American); Dean-Smith, 85 (English); and Greig and
Keith, 57-58 (Scottish).

The five tunes given here are related, four of them very
closely. Only the Fish tune diverges. In order to save repeti-
tion of references, the related tunes for the group consisting
of the Grindell, Moore, Britton, and Pierce tunes are given
here: SAA, 20; SSC, 122; Sharp 1, 148 (C), 149 (D and E),
146 (distant), and 147 (distant); AA, 124; DV, 574, No. 20
(E, L, and O); EO, 39, 40; BES, 139 (not too close); BI, 87.
Obviously this tune group is very widespread and its correla-
tion with the Child 75 text is great.

A

*Sent by Mrs. Sarah Taylor of New Bedford, Massachusetts,
as sung by her "Grandpa Jessup." Mrs. Taylor wrote that
"Lord Lovell" was "Grandpa Jessup's" favorite. This she
learned when a little girl.*

H. H. F., Collector
January 5, 1951

Structure: A B C D D (2,2,2,2,2); Rhythm A; Contour: arc;
Scale: hexachordal

t.c F. Note the 9/8 measure before the end.

Lord Lovell

Lord Lovell he stood by his castle gate
  A-combing his milk-white steed
When along came his Lady Nancy Bell
  A-wishing her lover God speed, speed, speed.

Lord Lovel

Tr. M. O.

Lord Lov - el he stood at his cas - tle gate A -
comb-ing his milk - y-white steed, When 'long came La - dy
Nan - cy Belle A - wish-ing her lov - er good
speed, speed, speed, A - wish-ing her lov - er good speed!

"Oh, where are you going, Lord Lovell?" she cried.
"Oh, where are you going?" cried she.
"I'm going," Lord Lovell answered her,
"Strange countries for to see, see, see,
Strange countries for to see."

"How long will you be gone, Lord Lovell?" she said,
"How long will you be gone?" said she.
"A year or two or three at the most,
Then I'll return to my Lady Nancy, see, see,
I'll return to my Lady Nancy."

Now Lord Lovell had been gone but a year and a day
Strange countries for to see
When alone in his heart he longed for to see
His own little Lady Nancy, see, see,
He longed for his Lady Nancy.

He called for his groom to saddle his horse
And he rode with all his speed;
He rode all day and ride all night

Until he reached London Town
And there he heard St. Patrick's bell
And people all gathered around, around, around,
And people all gathered around.

"Is anyone dead?" Lord Lovell, he said,
"Is anyone dead?" said he.
"Our Lady is dead," the people all said,
"We call her our Lady Nancy, see, see,
We call her our Lady Nancy."

"Oh, why did she die?" Lord Lovell did cry,
"Oh, why did she die?" cried he.
"She died of grief, it is our belief,
A-wanting her heart's desire, desire;
A-wanting her heart's desire."

They placed her in the old churchyard
Soon Lord Lovell was placed close by her
While out of her boosum there grew a white rose,
While out of his back bone a briar, a briar.

The rose and the briar they grew and entwined
Until they reached the old church tower.
They grew and entwined in each other's pure mind
A-longing their heart's desire;
A-longing their heart's desire.

B

*Sung by Mrs. Jessie Carpenter Grindell of Providence,
Rhode Island, as she learned it as a small child.*

M. Olney, Collector
January 29, 1945

Lord Lovel

Lord Lovel he stood at his castle gate
A-combing his milky-white steed,

When 'long came Lady Nancy Belle
A-wishing her lover good speed, speed, speed,
A-wishing her lover good speed!

"And where are you going, Lord Lovel?" said she;
"And where are you going?" said she.
"I'm going, my dear Lady Nancy Belle,
Strange countries for to see, see, see,
Strange countries for to see."

"And when will you be back?" says she;
"And when will you be back?"
"In a year or two or three at the most
I'll return to you, fair ladee, ladee;
I'll return to you, fair ladee."

He had not been gone but a year and a day
Strange countries for to see
When languishing thoughts came into his head:
Lady Nancy Belle he must see, see, see;
Lady Nancy Belle he must see.

He rode and he rode on his milk-white steed
Till he came to London town,
And there he heard St. Barna's bells
And the people a-mourning around, 'round, 'round,
And the people a-mourning around.

"Is anybody dead?" Lord Lovel said he;
"Is anybody dead?" said he.
"My lord's daughter's dead," a lady replied,
"And some call her Lady Nancee, -cee, -cee,
And some call her Lady Nancee."

He ordered the grave to be opened forthwith
And the shroud to be folded down,
And then he kissed the clay-cold lips

Till the tears came trickling down, down, down,
Till the tears came trickling down.

Lady Nancy Belle died as you might say today;
Lord Lovel, he died as tomorrow;
And out of her bosom there grew a red rose,
And out of Lord Lovel's, a briar, briar, briar,
And out of Lord Lovel's, a briar.

They grew and they grew till they reached the church top,
And then they couldn't grow any higher;
And there they entwined in a true lovers' knot,
Which true lovers always admire, -mire, -mire;
Which true lovers always admire.

C

*As sung by Mrs. Lena Bourne Fish of East Jaffrey, New
Hampshire, who learned it from her grandfather. Her
address was furnished by Mrs. Carl L. Schrader, Chairman
of Fine Arts, General Federation of Women's Clubs.*

M. Olney, Collector
May 8, 1940

Structure: A B C D^1 D^2 (2,2,2,3,2); Rhythm C and D; Contour: undulating; Scale: major

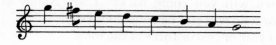

t.c. F.

For mel. rel. see SAA, 59 ("The Golden Vanity"); and EO,
41 (distant—note the octave leap).

Lord Lovel

Lord Lovel stood at his castle gate,
Combing his milk-white steed,
When along came Lady Nancy Bell,

Lord Lovel

Tr. H. E. F. B.

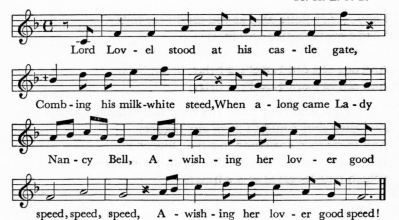

Lord Lov - el stood at his cas - tle gate,
Comb - ing his milk-white steed, When a - long came La - dy
Nan - cy Bell, A - wish - ing her lov - er good
speed, speed, speed, A - wish - ing her lov - er good speed!

A-wishing her lover good speed, speed, speed,
A-wishing her lover good speed.

"Where are you going?" Lady Nancy said.
"Are you going far?" said she.
"I am going, my dear Lady Nancy Bell,
Strange countries for to see, to see,
Strange countries for to see."

"When will you come back?" Lady Nancy said.
"How long will you be gone?" said she.
"In a year or two or three at the most
I'll return to you, Lady Nancy, -cee, -cee,
I'll return to you, Lady Nancy."

He had not been gone but a year and a day
Strange countries for to see,
When languishing thoughts came into his mind,
Lady Nancy Bell he would see, see, see,
Lady Nancy Bell he would see.

He rode, he rode on his milk-white steed,
Till he came to London town;
There he heard St. Vernon's bells,
And the people all a-mourning around, around,
And the people all a-mourning around.

"Is anybody dead?" Lord Lovel said.
"And who is it, pray tell me."
"A lord's daughter is buried today,
The rich and fair Lady Nancy, -cee, -cee,
The rich and fair Lady Nancy."

He ordered the grave to be opened forthwith,
And the shroud to be folded down.
Then he kissed her clay-cold lips
Till the tears came trickling down, down, down,
Till the tears came trickling down.

Lady Nancy died the same as today,
Lord Lovel on the morrow;
Out of Lady Nancy's grave sprang a rose,
And out of Lord Lovel's a briar, sweet briar,
And out of Lord Lovel's a briar.

They grew till they reached the churchyard top;
There they could grow no higher.
They entwined there in a true lover's knot
That true lovers always admire, admire,
That true lovers always admire.

D

Mrs. Frederic P. Lord of Hanover, New Hampshire, loaned for copying a manuscript in the family heritage of the Rogers family, formerly of Plymouth, New Hampshire, now of Long Beach, California. Among early forebears was Peabody Nathaniel Rogers, a graduate of Dartmouth in 1816, who became a lawyer and an abolitionist in Concord, where he published a paper called The Herald. *Because of his independent views, he and his family were ostracized in the community; he excommunicated the church in Concord! These songs were taught either by the mother from Pennsylvania, Ruth Dodd Luellen, or the father, Daniel Farrand Rogers, who may have learned them from his father, Peabody Nathaniel Rogers, born in 1794. Copied literatim et punctatim.*

Lord Lovel

Lord Lovel he stood in the castle gate
A-combin' his milk-white steed,
Lady Nancy, she came a-ridin' by,
A-wishin' her lover good speed, speed, speed,
A-wishin' her lover good speed.

"Oh where are you going, Lady Nancy?" she said,
"Oh! where are you going?" cried she.
"I'm going away from my Nancy Bell," dear
Strange countries for to see, see, see,
Strange countries for to see.

"When will you be back?" Lady Nancy, she said
"When will you be back?" cried she,
"In a year or two or three at most
I'll be back to my Lady Nancee, cee, cee,
I'll be back to my Lady Nancee."

He hadn't been gone but a year and a day,
Strange countries for to see,
When a languishing thought came into his mind,
His Nancy Bell he must see, see, see,
His Nancy Bell he must see.

So he rode and he rode all on his white steed,
Till he came to London town;

And there he heard St. Sepulchre's bell
And the people all mournin' around, round, round,
And the people all mournin' around.

"Is anyone dead?" Lord Lovel he said,
"Is anyone dead?" cried he.
"The Lord's daughter is dead," the people said,
And her name it is called Nancee, cee, cee
And her name it is called Nancee.

He ordered the tomb to be opened straightway,
And the shroud to be folded down,
And he kissed Lady Nancy's clay cold brow,
And the tears came a-trick-el-in' down, down, down,
And the tears came a-trick-el-in' down.

Lady Nancy she died as it were today,
Lord Lovel he died tomorrow;
Lady Nancy she died of pure true love,
Lord Lovel he died of sorrow, rorrow, rorrow,
Lord Lovel he died of sorrow.

Lady Nancy was buried all in the churchyard,
Lord Lovel was buried right by her,
And out of her grave there grew a red rose,
And out of her lover's a brier, rier, rier,
And out of her lover's a brier.

They grew and they grew to the steeple's top,
Till they couldn't grow any higher;
And there they entwined a true lover's knot
For true lovers to admire, mire, mire,
For true lovers to admire.

E

*The following words were taken down by Mrs. Bertha J.
Kneeland of Searsport, Maine, in 1914, from the singing of
her father-in-law, James Henry Kneeland, whose grandfather*

Edward Kneeland came to Cape Jellison from Boston about 1785. Frank E. Kneeland states that "This was much sung by Grandmothers Crockett and Kneeland."

M. Olney, Collector
July 17, 1941

Lord Lovel

Lord Lovel, he stood at his castle gate,
Combing his milk-white steed
When up came Lady Nancy Belle
To wish her lover God-speed—
To wish her lover God-speed.

"Where are you going, Lord Lovel?" she said.
"O, where are you going?" said she.
"I'm going, my Lady Nancy Belle,
Strange countries for to see—
Strange countries for to see."

"When will you be back, Lord Lovel?" she said,
"O, when will you come back?" said she.
"In a year or two, or three at the most,
I'll return to my fair Nancy—
I'll return to my fair Nancy."

But he had not been gone a year and a day,
Strange countries for to see,
When languishing thoughts came into his head,
Lady Nancy Belle he would go to see—
Lady Nancy Belle he would go to see.

So he rode and he rode on his milk-white steed
Till he came to London town,
And there he heard Saint Pancras' bells
And the people all mourning 'round—
And the people all mourning 'round.

"O, what is the matter?" Lord Lovel, he said.
"O, what is the matter?" said he.
"A lord's lady is dead," a woman replied,
"And some call her Lady Nancy—
And some call her Lady Nancy."

So he ordered the grave to be opened wide,
And the shroud, he turned down,
And there he kissed her clay-cold lips
Till the tears came trickling down—
Till the tears came trickling down.

Lady Nancy, she died as it might be today,
Lord Lovel, he died as tomorrow;
Lady Nancy, she died out of pure, pure grief,
Lord Lovel, he died out of sorrow—
Lord Lovel, he died out of sorrow.

Lady Nancy was laid in St. Pancras' Church,
Lord Lovel was laid in the choir,
And out of her bosom there grew a red rose,
And out of her lover's a briar—
And out of her lover's a briar.

They grew and they grew to the church steeple top,
And then they could grow no higher,
So there they entwined in a true lovers' knot
For all lovers true to admire—
For all lovers true to admire.

F

*Sent by Mrs. Marjorie Porter of Plattsburg, New York, as
learned in her family, formerly of Basin Harbor, Vermont.*
                              H. H. F., *Collector*
                              Spring, 1935

Lord Lovell

Lord Lovell he stood at his castle gate
A-combing his milk-white steed.
Lady Nancy Bell she came riding by
And wished her lover good-speed, good-speed,
And wished her lover good-speed, good-speed.

"Oh, where are you going, Lord Lovell," said she,
"Oh, where are you going," said she.
"I'm going away," Lord Lovell did say,
"Strange countries for to see-see-see,
Strange countries for to see."

Oh, he'd scarcely been gone twelve months and a day
Strange countries for to see,
Before the thot came o'er his mind
Lady Nancy Bell he'd go see-see-see,
Lady Nancy Bell he'd go see.

So he rode and he rode on his milk-white steed,
He rode till he reached the town,
And there he heard St. Varney's bell
And the people all mourning around-round-round,
And the people all mourning around.

"And what is the matter?" Lord Lovell said he,
"Oh, what is the matter?" said he.
"A lady has died but yesterday morn;
Some call her name Lady Nancy-Nancy,
Some call her name Lady Nancy."

So he ordered the coffin to be opened straightway,
And the corpse to be laid on the ground,
And then he kissed the clay-cold lips
And the tears came trickling down-down-down,
And the tears they came trickling down.

Lady Nancy she died as it might be today,
Lord Lovell he died on the morrow;
Lady Nancy died of pure, pure love,
Lord Lovell he died out of sorrow, sorrow, sorrow,
Lord Lovell he died out of sorrow.

Lady Nancy was buried in St. Mary's tomb,
Lord Lovell was buried beside her,
And out of her bosom there grew a red rose
And out of Lord Lovell's a briar-briar-briar,
And out of Lord Lovell's a briar.

And they grew and they grew till they reached the church
    tower,
And then they could grow no higher,
And there they entwined in a true lover's knot,
For all true lovers to admire-admire,
For all true lovers to admire.

G

Sent by Mrs. Minnie S. Havens, Chester, Vermont.

H. H. F., Collector
March 4, 1932

Lord Lovell

Lord Lovell he stood at the castle gate
  Combing his milk-white steed.
When along came Lady Nancy Bell
  A-wishing her lover good speed, speed, speed
    A-wishing her lover good speed.

Oh, when'll you be back Lord Lovell, she cried,
  Oh, when'll you be back, said she,
In a year or two or three at the most
  I'll return to my fair ladee, dee, dee
    I'll return to my fair ladee.

He'd scarcely been gone a year and a day
   Strange countries for to see,
When a languishing thought came into his heart,
   Lady Nancy Bell he must see, see, see,
      Lady Nancy Bell he must see.

So he rode and he rode on his milk-white steed
   'Till he came to London Town
And there he heard St. Varney's bell
   And the people all gathered around, 'round, 'round
      And the people all gathered around.

Is anybody dead, Lord Lovell he cried,
   Is anybody dead said he,
The Lord's daughter is dead, the people replied,
   Some call her the Lady Nancee, cee, cee,
      Some call her the Lady Nancee.

He ordered the grave to be opened forthwith,
   The shroud to be folded back,
And then he kissed the clay-cold lips
   And the tears they came trickling down, down, down,
      And the tears they came trickling down.

Lady Nancy she died as it might be today
   Lord Lovell he died tomorrow,
And over her bosom they planted a rose
   And over Lord Lovell's a brier, ier, ier,
      And over Lord Lovell's a brier.

They climbed and they climbed till they reached the church
     top,
   And when they could climb no higher
They twined themselves in a true Lovers Knot
   Which true lovers always admire, ire, ire,
      Which true lovers always admire.

H

As sung by Mrs. Belle Richards of Colebrook, New Hampshire.

M. Olney, Collector
July 21, 1943

Lord Lovel

Lord Lovel he stood at his castleyard gate
A-combing his milk-white steed,
When along came Lady Nancy Bell
A-wishing her lover good speed, speed, speed,
A-wishing her lover good speed.

"Oh, where are you going, Lord Lovel?" she said,
"Oh, where are you going?" said she.
"I'm going, Lady Nancy Bell,
Strange countries for to see, see, see,
Strange countries for to see."

"When will you be back, Lord Lovel?" she said,
"When will you be back?" said she.
"In a year or two or three at the most,
I'll return to my lovely Nancee, cee, cee,
I'll return to my lovely Nancee."

He hadn't been gone but a year and one day
Strange countries for to see,
When languishing thoughts came into his head,
Lady Nancy Bell he must go see, see, see,
Lady Nancy Bell he must go see.

So he rode and he rode on his milk-white steed
Till he came to Londontown,
And there he heard St. Varney's bells
And the people all mourning a-round, 'round, 'round,
And the people all mourning a-round.

"Is there anyone dead?" Lord Lovel, he said,
"Is there anyone dead?" said he.
"There's a lady dead," so the people all said,
"And they called her the Lady Nancee, cee, cee,
And they called her the Lady Nancee."

He ordered the grave to be opened forthwith
And the shroud to be folded down,
And there he kissed her clay-cold lips
And the tears came trickelling down, down, down,
And the tears they came trickelling down.

Lady Nancy she died the same as today;
Lord Lovel he died tomorrow.
Lady Nancee she died out of pure, pure grief,
And Lord Lovel he died out of sorrow, row, row,
And Lord Lovel he died out of sorrow.

Lady Nancee was buried in St. Clement's churchyard;
Lord Lovel was buried close by her,
And out of her bosom there grew a red rose,
And out of his backbone a briar, iar, iar,
And out of his backbone a briar.

They grew and they grew to the church steeple top
And they couldn't get up any higher,
And there they got twined in a true lovers' knot,
Just the kind that young people admire, ire, ire,
Just the kind that young people admire.

1

*As sung by Mrs. Annie Tate Moore of Ellsworth Falls,
Maine, learned from her sister about sixty years ago.*

M. Olney, Collector
June 22, 1941

Structure: A B C D D (2,2,2,2,2); Rhythm A; Contour: arc; Scale: hexachordal

t.c. D. Note the 9/8 measure before the end.

Lord Lovel

Tr. M. O.

Lord Lov - el he stood at his cas - tle gate A-

comb-ing his milk - y white steed When a - long came

La - dy Nan - cy Belle A - wish-ing her lov- er good

speed, speed, speed, A - wish-ing her lov- er good speed.

Lord Lovel

Lord Lovel he stood at his castle gate
A-combing his milky-white steed,
When along came Lady Nancy Belle
A-wishing her lover good speed, speed, speed,
A-wishing her lover good speed.

"Oh, where are you going, Lord Lovel?" she said;
"Oh, where are you going?" said she.
"I'm going afar away from home,
Strange countries for to see, see, see,
Strange countries for to see."

"When will you be back, Lord Lovel?" she said;
"When will you be back?" said she.
"In a year or two or three at the most,
I'll return to my Lady Nancee, cee, cee,
I'll return to Lady Nancee."

He had not been gone but a year and a day
Strange countries for to see,
When languishing thoughts came into his head,
Lady Nancee he would see, see, see,
Lady Nancee he would see.

He rode and he rode on his milky-white steed
Till he came to London town,
And there he heard the village bells
And the people all mourning around, 'round, 'round,
And the people all mourning around.

"Is anyone dead?" Lord Lovel, he said,
"Is anyone dead?" said he.
"A lady is dead!" the people all said,
And they called her the Lady Nancee, cee, cee,
And they called her the Lady Nancee.

He ordered the grave to be opened wide
And the shroud to be folded down,
And there he kissed her clay-cold lips
Till the tears came trickling down, down, down,
Till the tears came trickling down.

Lady Nancy died as 'twas yesterday,
Lord Lovel he died as tomorrow;
And out of her breast there grew a red rose
But out of Lord Lovel's a briar, briar, briar,
But out of Lord Lovel's a briar.

They grew and they grew to the top of the church
Until they could grow no higher:

And there they entwined in a true lover's knot,
Such as only young lovers admire, mire, mire,
Such as only young lovers admire.

J

*Sung by Mrs. Laura Britton of Putney, Vermont, as learned
from her mother, who was Martha Sleeper, born in Chelsea,
Vermont.*

M. Olney, Collector
January 8, 1945

Structure: A B C D¹ D² (2,2,2,2,2); Rhythm A; Contour:
arc; Scale: major

t.c. D.

Lord Lovel

Tr. M. O.

Lord Lov-el he stood at his cas-tle gate A-
comb-ing his milk-white steed, When a-long came La-dy
Nan-cy-belle, A-wish-ing her lov-er good
speed, speed, speed, A-wish-ing her lov-er good speed.

Lord Lovel

Lord Lovel he stood at his castle gate
A-combing his milk-white steed,
When along came Lady Nancybelle,
A-wishing her lover good speed, speed, speed,
A-wishing her lover good speed.

"Oh, where are you going, Lord Lovel?" she said;
"Oh, where are you going?" said she.
"I'm going, I'm going I know not where,
Strange countries for to see, see, see,
Strange countries for to see."

He hadn't been gone but a little over a year
Strange countries for to see,
Before a strange thought entered into his head,
Lady Nancy for to see, see, see,
Lady Nancy for to see.

So he rode, he rode on his milk-white steed
'Til he came to London town,
And there he heard the church bells ring
And the people go moaning around, 'round, 'round,
The people go moaning around.

"Who's dead, who's dead?" Lord Lovel, he said;
"Who's dead, who's dead?" said he.
"The princess is dead," the lady replied;
"Some call her Lady Nancee, cee, cee,
Some call her Lady Nancee."

He ordered the grave to be opened forthwith
And the shroud to be folded down,
And there he kissed her clay-cold cheek
While the tears came trickerling down, down, down,
While the tears came tricklin' down.

Lady Nancy she died the same as today;
Lord Lovel he died tomorrow,
And from her heart there grew a white rose,
And from Lord Lovel's a briar, briar, briar,
And from Lord Lovel's a briar.

They grew, they grew till they reached the church top
Where they could grow no higher,
And there they tied a true lover's knot
That true lovers always admire, mire, mire,
That true lovers always admire.

K

Sent by Miss Amy Perkins of Rutland, Vermont. As sung by her grandmother, Eliza A. (Craigue) Fisher of Reading, Vermont.

H. H. F., Collector
Fall, 1931

Lord Lovell

Lord Lovell, he stood at his own castle gate
A-combing his milk-white steed,
When up came Lady Nancy Bell
To wish her lover good speed, speed, speed,
To wish her lover good speed.

"Oh, where are you going, Lord Lovell?" she said;
"Oh, where are you going?" said she.
"I'm going away, Miss Nancy Bell,
Strange countries for to see, see, see,
Strange countries for to see."

"When will you be back, Lord Lovell?" she said;
"When will you be back?" said she.
"A year or two or three at the most
I'll return to my Lady Nancee, cee, cee,
I'll return to my Lady Nancy."

A year and a day had passed away;
He returned to Fair London Town
And there he heard St. Anthony's bell
And the people all mourning around, 'round, 'round,
And the people all mourning around.

"Oh, who is dead?" Lord Lovell, he said;
"Oh, who is dead?" said he.
"A lord's daughter is dead," an old woman said;
"Some call her the Lady Nancee, cee, cee,
Some call her the Lady Nancy."

He ordered the grave to be opened forthwith
And the shroud to be folded down.
And there he kissed her clay cold lips
And the tears they came tricklying down, down, down,
And the tears they came tricklying down.

Lady Nancy was buried in the green churchyard;
Lord Lovell was buried near by her.
And out of her bosom there grew a red rose
And out of her lover's, a briar, iar, iar,
And out of her lover's a briar.

They grew and they grew to the church steeple top
Till they could not grow any higher,
And there they entwined in a double bow knot
For all lovers true to admire, ire, ire,
For all lovers true to admire.

L

Text and tune contributed by Mrs. John Pierce of Spring-
field, Vermont, as learned from her mother, Alice Maude
Crawford. Printed in Vermont Folk-Songs & Ballads, *215.*

Structure: A B C D¹ D² (4,4,4,4,4); Rhythm D, inverted;
Contour: arc; Scale: major

t.c. E-flat.

Lord Lovell

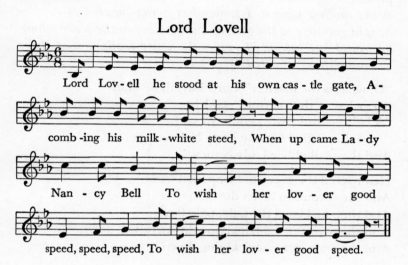

Lord Lov-ell he stood at his own cas-tle gate, A-
comb-ing his milk-white steed, When up came La-dy
Nan-cy Bell To wish her lov-er good
speed, speed, speed, To wish her lov-er good speed.

Lord Lovell

Lord Lovell, he stood at his own castle gate,
A-combing his milk-white steed,
When up came Lady Nancy Bell
To wish her lover good speed, speed, speed,
To wish her lover good speed.

"O, where are you going, Lord Lovell?" she said,
"O, where are you going?" said she.
"I'm going away, Miss Nancy Bell,
Strange countries for to see, see, see,
Strange countries for to see."

"When will you be back, Lord Lovell?" she said,
"When will you be back?" said she.
"A year or two or three at the most
I'll return to my Lady Nancee, cee, cee,
I'll return to my Lady Nancy."

[*Mrs. Pierce writes, "There is an evident hiatus in the tale
as my mother sang it. I remember being puzzled as to why
he said goodbye to the girl, and rode away to the place where
he found her buried; I evidently never realized that there
was something omitted."*]

"O, what is the matter?" Lord Lovell, he said,
"O, what is the matter?" said he.
"A lady is dead," the people all said,
"And they called her the Lady Nancee, cee, cee,
And they called her Lady Nancy."

He ordered the grave to be opened wide,
And the shroud to be let down,
And then he kissed the pale, pale face,
And the tears came a-tricklying down, down, down,
And the tears came a-tricklying down.

And out of her bosom there grew a red rose,
And out of her lover's, a briar, iar, iar,
And out of her lover's a briar.

They grew and they grew till they reached the church top
Till they couldn't grow up no higher;
Then they twined themselves into a true lovers' knot
For all lovers true to admire, ire, ire,
For all lovers true to admire.

M

*Recorded in Wardsboro, Vermont, as remembered by
George Farnham, 77 years old, from the singing of his*

mother, Lydia French Farnham, born in Windsor, Vermont.

George Brown, Collector
August 28, 1930

Lord Lovell

Lord Lovell, he stood at his castle gate
A-combing his milk-white steed
When along came his lady, Nancy Bell,
A-wishing her lover God-speed, -speed, -speed
A-wishing her lover God-speed.

"Oh, where are you going, Lord Lovell?" she said.
"Oh, where are you going?" said she.
"I'm going, my Lady Nancy Bell,
Strange countries for to see, see, see
Strange countries for to see."

The Lass of Roch Royal
(Child 76)

As David C. Fowler has indicated (*JAF*, 1958, 553-63), "The Lass of Roch Royal" recounts the medieval tale of "The Accused Queen." Anny goes to find her true love, Gregor, carrying their young child in her arms. Gregor is asleep when she arrives at his door. His mother, thinking she is a witch, rejects her with the information that Gregor has a new love. Even the love tokens that Anny carries are not enough to convince the old lady. Before long, Gregor awakens, learns what has happened, and is furious with his mother. But it is too late. He rushes off, only to come upon Anny's funeral, which he stops in order to kiss the corpse. Texts of this song are not at all easy to find in America. Josiah Combs, *Folk-Songs des Etats-Unis* (Paris, 1926), 134, and J. Harrington Cox, *Folk-Songs of the South* (Cambridge, Mass., 1925), 83, discovered rather full examples of Child D from West Virginia, and it is in the Southeast that the song is known. The fragment from George Edwards is unique for the rest of the nation and, of course, is woefully abbreviated. The lines printed below follow Child A (compare Edwards' name for the hero and his lines 3-4 with Child A, stanza 1). As Child A is not found in America and as Edwards knew a number of other songs (Child 25, 96, 176, for example) unknown here, it may well be that someone in his family had access to the Child collection in one way or other.

Child 76 has been abused by American collectors eager to

swell the ranks of the traditional ballads discovered in this
country. Usually what has been found is only the stanzas
that begin,

> "Who will shoe my pretty little feet
> And who will glove my hand,
> And who will kiss my red, red lips
> When you're in some far off land?"

These lines are part of the floating lyric material of Anglo-
American song and turn up in ballads as varied as "The
Wagoner's Lad," "Lord Randal," "James Harris," and
"John Henry." Usually they are found mixed with equally
common lines about "lonesome turtle doves," "green wil-
lows," and "ten thousand miles in Scotland, France, or
Spain" and appear under a variety of titles like "A True
Lover's Farewell," "A Cold Winter's Night," or "Careless
Love." Such lyric matter belongs to no one song and cannot
be used to identify texts. Originally it must have wandered
into Child 76 much as it has wandered into ten thousand
other places.

The American bibliography for "The Lass of Roch
Royal" is in Coffin, 79-81. There also are many references
for the "shoe-my-foot" lines. See Greig and Keith, 59 f., for
Scottish material, and Riverside, RLP 12-627 (*The English
and Scottish Popular Ballads,* Volume 4, Side 1) for a recording of Ewan MacColl singing a version recently collected
in Wiltshire, England.

A

*Fragment recalled by George Edwards of Burlington, Ver-
mont, as sung by his grandfather of Seaton, East Riding,
Yorkshire, England.*

> H. H. F., Collector
> October 16, 1934

The Lass of Rock Royal

"Or who will my children's father be?"

"Who will comb my bonnie hair
And from whence will come the comb?"

Fair Isabelle of Rock Royal,
She dreaming as she lay,

[Her lover's name was Gregory.]

B

As sung by Mrs. Mabel White Lansing, born in North Attle-boro, Massachusetts. She learned this ballad from her mother, Mary Jane Montgomery. Mrs. Lansing is a direct descendant of the Bradfords, the Whites, and the Curtises of Bristol and Plymouth Counties, Massachusetts.

M. Olney, Collector
August 27, 1944

Structure: A¹ A²(tr) B C (2,2,2,2); Rhythm divergent; Contour: approaching an arc; Scale: major

t.c. E-flat.

For mel. rel. see DV, 575, No. 21(A); RO 1, 121—neither very close.

Tr. M. O.

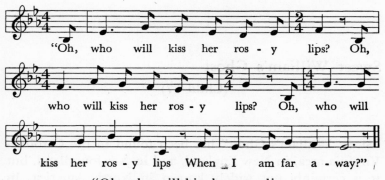

"Oh, who will kiss her ros-y lips? Oh,
who will kiss her ros-y lips? Oh, who will
kiss her ros-y lips When I am far a-way?"

"Oh, who will kiss her rosy lips,
Oh, who will kiss her rosy lips,
Oh, who will kiss her rosy lips
When I am far away?"

Sweet William's Ghost

(Child 77)

"Sweet William's Ghost" has been found in the Carolina-Virginia area, in New England, and in Newfoundland, but it is certainly not widely known in North America. In Britain, it has become rare, too, although Child prints seven versions. There is an analogous song, "The Betrothed in the Grave," which in Child's words is "one of the most beautiful and celebrated of the Scandinavian ballads."

Behind the song lies a Germanic folk belief that a deceased lover cannot be at rest in the land of the dead when he still has an earthly tie. The revenant comes to ask back his unfulfilled troth. The crowing of the cocks, white or gray, red, and black, is the signal for his return to the coffin. Margaret, who cannot follow her lover into the grave, dies in sorrow. Child, II, 226-29, gives a full discussion of the superstitions involved.

Flanders A, from *The Green Mountain Songster,* is like Child C, from the Motherwell MS, in general plot outline, although there are marked differences in the two texts. Both, however, do include the three unwed girls and their three children standing in the grave, but where the Child text has hellhounds Flanders A has three maids to guide the dead man's soul. Flanders B is a close replica of Child A, which is not the usual American form of the ballad. No mention is made in this text of the occupants of the grave; the coffin is merely too "meet" for Margaret to get in.

Coffin, 81-82, gives an American bibliography. Child, II,

226 f., discusses British variations and the analogues. Dean-Smith does not list the song at all.

A

Copied literatim et punctatim from page 34 of The Green Mountain Songster, *which is in the possession of Harold Rugg at the Baker Memorial Library in Hanover, New Hampshire. This Songster was compiled by a Revolutionary soldier and published in the town of Sandgate in 1823. Printed in* Vermont Folk-Songs & Ballads, *240.*

H. H. F., Collector
1930

Lady Margaret and Sweet William

LADY Margaret sat in her own bowery all alone,
And under her bowry east window she heard three pitiful
groans;
Oh, is it my father dear, she said, or is it my brother John,
Or is it my loving dear William from Scotland newly come
home?

It is not your father, he said, nor is it your brother John,
But is your loving dear William from Scotland newly come
home.
Oh have you brought me any gold, she said, or have you
brought me any fee,
Or have you bro't any fine linnen from Scotland home to
me?

I have not bro't you any gold, he said nor have I bro't you
any fee,
But I've brought you my winding sheet 'tis rotted off from
me;
Give me my troth Lady Margaret, he said, I'll give thee
thine again,

For the longer I tarry and talk with you the sharper'll be
  my pain.

I will not give you your troth she said nor you give mine
  to me,
Until you carry me to fair Scotland your bowry for to see.
My bowry 'tis a poor bowry it is both deep and dim;
My bowry 'tis a poor bowry to put a fair lady in.

I will not give you your troth she said nor will I have mine
  again,
Until you kiss my merry merry lips or wed me with a ring.
I cannot kiss your merry, merry lips, by breath it is so strong,
My face it is all worm-eaten, I am no living man.

She pulled up her petticoat, almost unto her knee,
And in a cold and a winter's night the pale ghost follow'd
  she;
Oh who are these, sweet William, she said, are standing at
  your head?
They're three pretty maids, Lady Margaret, he said, that I
  refus'd to wed.

Oh who are these, sweet William, she said, are standing at
  your feet?
They're three children, Lady Margaret, he said, that I refus'd to keep.
Oh who are these, sweet William, she said, are standing by
  your side?
They're three pretty maids, Lady Margaret, he said, waiting
  my soul to guide.

The first is for my drunkenness, the second's for my pride,
The third is for my false swearing and wandering in the
  night;
Give me my troth, Lady Margaret, he said, I'll give thee
  thine again,

For the longer I tarry and talk with you the sharper'll be
my pain.

She had a handkerchief in her hand she spread it on the
ground,
Saying, here is your faith and troth William, God lay your
body down;
She had a willow in her hand, she laid it across his breast,
Saying, here is your faith and troth, William, I wish your
soul at rest.

So here is your faith and troth William, and give me mine
again,
But if you're dead and gone to hell in hell you must remain.

B

*Copied literatim et punctatim by H. H. F. from a compila-
tion of 400 pages of numbered issues of* The Charms of
Melody: *or* Siren Medley, *printed by J. & J. Carrick, Bachelor's Walk, Dublin. The watermark on the title page reads*
GREAT NEWTON, *with the date 1818. Copies are available at the Boston Athenaeum; the John Hay Library at
Brown University (60 pages, dated 1824, beginning with
volume 1, page 1); and at the Library of Congress.*

H. H. F., *Collector*
August 1, 1958

Margaret and Willy.
An Old Scotch Ballad

There came a ghoft to Marg'ret's door,
With many a grievous groan,
And ay he twirled at the pin,
But anfwer made fhe none.

"Is that my father Philip?
"Or is't my brother John?

"Or is't my true love Willy,
"From Scotland new come home?"

" 'Tis not thy father Philip,
"Nor yet thy brother John;
"But 'tis thy true love Willy,
"From Scotland new come home.

"O fweet Marg'ret! O dear Marg'ret!
"I pray thee fpeak to me;
"Give me my faith and troth, Marg'ret,
"As I gave it to thee."

"Thy faith and troth thou's never get,
"Nor yet will I thee lend,
"Till that thou come within my bow'r,
"And kifs my cheek and chin."

"If I fhould come within thy bow'r,
"I am no earthly man;
"And fhou'd I kifs thy rofy lips,
"Thy days will not be lang.

"O fweet Marg'ret! O dear Marg'ret!
"I pray thee fpeak to me;
"Give me my faith and troth, Marg'ret,
"As I gave it to thee."

"Thy faith and troth thou's never get,
"Nor yet will I thee lend.
"Till you take me to yon kirk-yard,
"And wed me with a ring."

"My bones are buried in yon kirk-yard,
"A far beyond the fea;
"And it is but my fpirit, Marg'ret,
"That's now fpeaking to thee."

She ftretch'd out her lily-white hand,
And for to do her beft,

"Hae there's your faith and troth, Willy,
"God fend your foul good reft."

Now fhe has kilted her robes of green
A piece below her knee,
And aw the live-lang winter night
The dead corpfe follow'd fhe.

"Is there room at your head, Willy?
"Or any room at your feet?
"Or any room at your fide, Willy,
"Wherein that I may creep?"

"There's no room at my head, Marg'ret;
"There's no room at my feet;
"There's no room at my fide, Marg'ret.
"My coffin's made fo meet."

Then up and crew the red, red cock,
And up then crew the grey;
" 'Tis time, 'tis time, my dear Marg'ret,
"That you were going away."

No more the ghoft to Marg'ret faid,
But, with a grievous groan,
He vanifh'd in a cloud of mift,
And left her all alone.

"O ftay, my only true love, ftay,"
The conftant Marg'ret cry'd;
Wan grew her cheeks, fhe clos'd her een,
Stretch'd her foft limbs, and dy'd.

The Unquiet Grave

(Child 78)

"The Unquiet Grave" is based on the old, old folk belief that excessive grief disturbs the rest of the dead. However, all texts recovered for this song date from the nineteenth century or later. Most of them are quite brief, and it is likely the original ballad told a much longer tale.

The song is seldom found in the New World. A half a dozen or so texts have been recorded from the South and from northern New England and Newfoundland. The Flanders version is an abbreviated form of the tradition represented in Cecil Sharp's *100 English Folk Songs* (New York, 1916), No. 24. It is also much like No. 23A in Elisabeth B. Greenleaf and Grace Y. Mansfield's *Ballads and Sea Songs of Newfoundland* (Cambridge, Mass., 1924) and Child C, although the mourner is male and not female as in those texts.

For a start on the brief bibliography of this song, see Coffin, 82-83 (American) and Dean-Smith, 113 (English). It is almost unknown in Scotland.

Sung by Mrs. Lily Delorme of Starksboro, Vermont. Printed in Ballads Migrant in New England, *232.*

M. Olney, Marjorie Porter, Collectors
August 16, 1943

Structure: A¹ A² B A¹ (2,2,2,2); Rhythm divergent; Contour: arc; Scale: hexachordal

t.c. C. Note the small range (major sixth). Structure of the third verse: A B B A.

For mel. rel. see GN, 23: our line 3 is like its beginning.

Cold Blows the Winter's Winds

Tr. M. O.

Cold blows the win - ter's wind, sweet - heart, Cold blows the drops of rain; I nev - er had but one sweet - heart And in the green-wood she was slain.

4. "What do you want of me, sweet - heart?" What do you want of me, I pray? "One kiss, one kiss of your clay - cold lips And that is all I want of thee."

Cold Blows the Winter's Wind

Cold blows the winter's wind, sweetheart,
Cold blows the drops of rain;
I never had but one sweetheart
And in the greenwood she was slain.

I'll do as much for my sweetheart
As any young man may;
I'll sit all on her grave and mourn
A twelvemonth and a day.

A twelvemonth and a day being past,
Her ghost began to speak:
"Why sit upon my grave and mourn
And will not let me sleep?"

"What do you want of me, sweetheart?
What do you want of me, I pray?"
"One kiss, one kiss of your clay-cold lips
And that is all I want of thee."

"My lips are colder than clay, sweetheart,
My breath I'm sure is not strong.
If one kiss of my clay-cold lips you have,
Your time, it won't be long."

The Wife of Usher's Well

(Child 79)

The tradition of "The Wife of Usher's Well" is much confused, although most of the American texts are rather consistent in their similarity to Child D, from North Carolina. The British versions, now pretty much extinct, are generally incomplete or garbled. Child A and B give no motive for the return of the three sons nor do they describe the actions of the sons at home. C is nearly impossible to follow, although the return comes as a result of prayer as it does in D. Belden, 55-56, and Jane Zielonko, "Some American Variants of Child Ballads" (Master's thesis, Columbia University, 1945), 104 f., both discuss the manner in which the Child D tradition varies from the Child A-C texts. Belden seems certain the Child D tradition goes back to print, but he can offer no references. However, there is strong circumstantial evidence to back his feeling as the song is rare in Britain, widespread and relatively unvarying in this country.

In the light of these facts, the Flanders texts are immensely interesting. Flanders A is a close reproduction of Child A from *Minstrelsy of the Scottish Border* (1802), II, 111, and thus quite unusual for America. This brings up the possibility that it was learned directly from Sir Walter Scott's volume or from Child by someone in Mrs. Burditt's family. Flanders B, which does not seem to be a ghost story at all, but rather a sentimental love tale spiced with maternal devotion, is a remarkable find. Obviously it is near print; the trite language and the maudlin plot are proof enough of that. Originally, it may be related to the tradition of the garbled Child C from Shropshire where the boys are named Joe, Peter, and John, although names Malcolm, Jock, and Don seem Scottish or at least Scotch-Irish. It is actually a completely new song, not Child 79 at all, and no closer to its "progenitor" than many of the so-called secondary ballads.

L. C. Wimberly, *Folklore in the English and Scottish Popular Ballads* (Chicago, 1928), 226, discusses the themes of revenants, moralistic punishment, and transformation that are interwoven into the American texts. Coffin, 83-84, gives an American bibliography and summary. Dean-Smith does not list the song, although it appears in E. M. Leather's *The Folk-Lore of Herefordshire* (London, 1912), 198.

A

Sung by Mrs. Phyllis Burditt of Springfield, Vermont. Published in Ballads Migrant in New England, *64.*[1]

M. Olney, Collector
October 11, 1951

[1] When Mrs. Burditt resang this song for the LP record in 1953 (see Vol. I, p. 42), she varied stanza 5 as follows:

> Up then did crow the red, red cock
> And up and crew the gray;
> The eldest to the youngest said,
> " 'Tis time we were away."
> The cock he hadn't crowed but once
> And clapped his wings away
> When the youngest to the oldest said,
> "O brother, we must away!"

This variation is more like Child A, stanzas 9-10, than the original singing.

Tune is identical with B below (Mrs. Fish).

Structure: A B B A (4,4,4,4); Rhythm D; Contour: arc; Scale: hexatonic

t.c. B-flat; C for the Fish version.

For mel. rel. see Sharp 1, 153(E); EO, 46 (very distant); and possibly FCB4, 49(C), of which our tune is an expanded form.

The Wife of Usher's Well

Tr. M. O.

The Wife of Usher's Well

There lived a wife at Usher's Well
And a wealthy wife was she;
She had three stout and stalwart sons
And sent them o'er the sea.
They had not been a week from her,
A week but barely one,
When word came to the carline[2] wife
That her three sons were gone.

They had not been a week from her,
A week but barely three,
When word came to the carline wife
That her sons she'd never see.
"I wish the wind may never cease
Nor fishes in the flood,
Till my three sons come home to me
In earthly flesh and blood!"

It fell about the Martinmas,
When nights are long and mirk,[3]
The carline wife's three sons came home
And their hats were on the birk.[4]
It neither grew in syke[5] nor ditch,
Nor yet in any sheugh,[6]
But at the gates of Paradise
That birk grew fair enough.

"Blow up the fires, my maidens fair!
Bring water from the well!
For all my house shall feast this night
Since my three sons are well!"

[2] "carline": "old woman"
[3] "mirk": "dark"
[4] "birk": "birch" (associated with the dead)
[5] "syke": "marsh"
[6] "sheugh": "trench" or "ditch"

And she has made for them a bed—
She's made it long and wide;
And she's put her mantle round about,
Sat down at their bedside.

The cock he had not crowed but once
And clapped his wings away
When the youngest to the eldest said,
"Brother, we must away!"
Up then did crow the red, red cock
And up then crew the gray;
The eldest to the youngest said,
" 'Tis time we were away."

"The cock doth crow, the day doth dawn,
The channerin[7] worm doth chide;
Gin we be miss out of our place,
A sair pain we maun bide.
Fare you well, my mother dear!
Farewell to barn and byre! [8]
And fare you well, the bonny lass
That kindles my mother's fire!"

B

Sung by Mrs. Lena Bourne Fish of East Jaffrey, New Hampshire. It is an eight-line tune. On January 5, 1943 she sang an identical retake for H. H. F.

M. Olney, Collector
July 16, 1942

For annotation see A above, since the two tunes are identical.

[7] "channerin": "fretting"
[8] "byre": "cow stable"

The Wife at Usher's Well

Tr. M. O.

There lived a dame at Ush-er's Well And a come-ly dame was she. She had three brave and hard-y sons Who sailed the deep blue sea. Once on a voy-age they did go— So it has been told to me — When word came to this worth-y dame That her sons had been lost at sea.

Wife of Usher's Well

There lived a dame at Usher's well
And a comely dame was she.
She had three brave and hardy sons
Who sailed the deep blue sea.
Once on a voyage they did go—
So it has been told to me—

When word came to this worthy dame
That her sons had been lost at sea.

Now this poor dame did weep and mourn,
For her sons she did adore,
When told that her three sons were dead,
That she'd see them nevermore.
She vowed that she would eat no flesh
Nor drink a drop of wine
Till her three sons came home again
From across the foaming brine.

One morning as the cock did crow
Some one knocked on her door,
Which proved to be her hardy sons
Whom she thought she'd see no more.
She kissed them and embraced them too
As only mothers can
For she did love her manly sons—
Her Malcolm, Jock and Dan.

"I'll give each one a gift," said she,
"So ask me what you will,
For my lamp of faith is shining bright—
God's mercy liveth still;
For what is gold and land, my sons,
Or treasures rare?" quoth she.
"They'll not compare to my three sons
Which God has spared to me."

Malcolm asked for the family coat-of-arms—
Or so I have heard say—
And Jock desired the houses and lands
Beyond the castle brae.[1]
Said Dan, "I do not ask for gold,
But there's one thing I desire:

[1] "brae": "hill"

It's the hand of that bonny maid of thine
Who daily lights your fire."

"My son, do you love this maiden fair?"
"That I do with all my heart!"
"Then you shall wed this very day
And nevermore shall part.
We will have a merrie wedding, son;
We'll dance and sing and dine;
And drink a toast to your bonny bride
With mother's choicest wine."

Little Musgrave and Lady Barnard
(Child 81)

This ballad has a vigorous American oral tradition but, in spite of the fact that Phillips Barry, *British Ballads from Maine,* 173, reports his H version to have been learned in Scotland, seems to have died out in Britain. Here it is known everywhere, from Nova Scotia to Jamaica and west. Barry, *op. cit.,* 180 f., and Helen Pettigrew, *University of West Virginia Studies,* III, *Philological Papers,* II, 8 f., both spent much effort on the American heritage of Child 81. Barry feels there was a pre-American split in the tradition of the ballad, one form featuring the "away, Musgrave, away" lines and the "bugle-blowing" scene, the other retaining mention of King Henry. The Henry type he believes to date back to the time of Henry VIII and to be the progenitor of almost all the American texts. The "away, Musgrave" type, he feels, gave birth to the Anglo-Scottish texts and a few late American arrivals. Pettigrew attacks this thesis vigorously, among other things, attributing the visit to King Henry to romanticization and citing a host of American texts, such as the Flanders ones below, that retain "bugle-blowing" scenes. Whoever is right, one thing seems sure: Barry was not far wrong in stating the song has been in America a long time and that the texts here are more vivid and generally better than those in Child, some of which are pretty old.

The Flanders texts demonstrate Barry's two types. Flan-

195

ders A includes a strong "bugle-blowing" scene, the "away" lines (stanzas 18-20), and opens with a church-gathering like Child A, C, H, and many of the southern American texts. This version is similar to the one in Belden, 58 (also printed in *British Ballads from Maine,* 177), but is unusual for the New World in its inclusion of Lady Barnard's effort to bribe the page as in Child C-F, H-L, and O. Edwards, it should be noted, wanted to leave these lines and some of the "bugle" material out (see the letter below). The Flanders B-J series is more typical of the northern tradition of the ballad and starts like Child D, E, K, L with a "ball-playing" scene. The "bugle-blowing" is presented, but briefly, and there are no "away, Musgrave" lines.

See Coffin, 84-86, for the bibliography of the American texts and summaries of the scholarship done on the song. It is interesting that American versions do not mention any past relationship between the lovers, although Musgrave needs no encouragement when the Lady flirts with him in one Southeastern text. He embraces her at once. *PMLA,* XXXIX, 455 f., contains a report on the Jamaican tradition of Child 81. The ballad as known in the West Indies is closer to Child A-C than it is to the American material.

In Act V, scene 3, of Francis Beaumont's *The Knight of the Burning Pestle,* Merrythought quotes lines from the song.

The seven tunes given are related except for the Edwards tune, which seems separate. The rest fall into two related groups: 1) Colsie and Walker, and 2) Syphers, Merrill, Finnemore, and Burditt. The following tunes show general relationship to the second of these related groups: Sharp 1, 166 (D), 181(L); and BES, 150. The New England tunes seem more closely related to the second group, while those in the collections from the southern United States seem largely to belong to another family exemplified by the majority of the tunes in Sharp 1.

A

As printed in Ballads Migrant in New England, *86: George Edwards says, in giving this song, in typewritten form, that it is "just as I always used it, and as I always heard it, with the one exception. I have omitted the word 'little' immediately preceding the name 'Mottha Grow' wherever it occurs in the piece. It always seemed to me that the words crowded the music (if that is a proper way to express what I mean). I also did not like the impression the word conveyed, as it seemed to me rather to belittle the person to whom it is attached and also to give a mental picture of a boy or youth, instead of a man." See also the letter from Edwards below.*[1]

H. H. F., Collector
July 27, 1933

[1] This letter is revealing, as it demonstrates how and why an informant will change a song. The stanzas referred to are noted. Edwards' placing of them in the letter corresponds with their position in the text as he originally sent it.

Burlington, Vermont
December 9, 1933

Dear Mrs. Flanders:

About fifteen minutes ago I received a letter from Mrs. Fannie H. Eckstorm and containing a proof sheet of the "Lord Arnold" ballad that I sent to you, and which she has just had published in the Bangor Daily News.

She informs me that you requested her to do this and I want you to know how much I appreciate your thoughtfulness for this pleasure to me, also for her kindness in acceding to your request.

You will recollect that the copy I sent to you was as I used it many years ago. There are, however, six other verses that belong to this ballad as I learned it from my grandfather and which I have omitted for various reasons as follows:

There is a verse between the thirteenth and fourteenth stanzas, as your copy reads, that I sent to you, dealing with a promised reward from Lord Arnold to the foot page, if what he said was true, and which I thought altogether too generous for the services rendered and so left it out.

Again between the sixteenth and seventeenth verses a stanza that has to do with the bugle call, which I noticed that Mrs. Eckstorm misses and asks about, and which I thought superfluous and hence did not use it.

[Footnote continues on page 198]

Structure: A B C^b D E^d (2,2,2,2,2); Rhythm D; Contour: arc; Scale: major

t.c. D-flat.

For mel. rel. see Sharp 1, 178(K), 164 (distant), possibly 172(H); BP, 32; possibly FCB4, 53(B).

Lord Arnold

Tr. M. O.

It was on one fine, one fine hol - i - day, The
fin - est day in the year, That
lit - tle Mot - tha Grow to the church did go, The
Ho - ly word to hear. The Ho - ly word to hear.

Then again, between the eighteenth and nineteenth verses, there are two stanzas missing which, owing to the sentiment expressed in them, I did not like to use in a mixed audience, the reason for which you will readily see when you read them.

The above missing verses I am sending to you with this letter, but the last two, which should come between the sixth and seventh verses, well, perhaps I will include them, but I am quite sure that you will think as I do that they are incongruous, and to me they seem to disrupt or at least to detract from the even progression of the theme of the ballad that runs so nicely from the beginning to its culmination.

In recording ballads on dictaphone, do you want the entire ballad or a verse from each?

Cordially,
/s/ Geo. Edwards.

Lord Arnold

It was on one fine, one fine holiday,
The finest day in the year,
That Mottha Grow to the church did go
The Holy Word to hear.
The Holy Word to hear.

(Repeat last line in each stanza.)

The ladies fine, they all came in,
In satin and in blue.
The last of them all was Lord Arnold's wife,
The finest of the whole crew.

She looked around, she looked around,
She look-ed him upon,
Saying, "Mottha Grow, to my home must go,
And along with me shall come."

"I dare not, I dare not," said Mottha Grow,
"I dare not for my life,
For I know by the rings on your fingers,
That you are Lord Arnold's wife."

"And what if I am Lord Arnold's wife,
And what is that to thee?
Lord Arnold has gone to the Hampshire Court,
King Henry for to see."

A little foot page, a-standing near,
Heard all they had to say,
Thought, "I will tell Lord Arnold of this
Before the break of day."

"O, gold your head shall crown," Lady Arnold said,
"And silver your feet shall be,
If you will not tell Lord Arnold of what was said
Between Mottha Grow and me." [1]

"O, gold will not crown my head," said he,
"Nor your silver will I take,
But I will tell Lord Arnold of this
Ere another day shall break." [1]

He had many long miles to go
And some of them he ran,
And when he came to a broken bridge,
He down on his breast and swam.

And when he came to the Hampshire Court,
So loudly he did ring,
And none so ready as Lord Arnold himself
To arise and let him in.

"Are either of my towers burned,
Or is my castle won,
Or is my fair lady brought to bed,
With a daughter or a son?"

"There are neither of your towers burned,
Nor is your castle won,
Neither is your fair lady brought to bed
With a daughter or a son."

"What news, what news, my little foot page,
What news have you brought to me?"
"I have brought you the news that Mottha Grow
Is at home with your fair lady."

"If this be a lie," Lord Arnold, he said,
"That you have told to me,
I will have a wooden gallows made,
And hanged you shall be."

"If this be a lie," said the little foot page,
"That I have brought to thee,
You need not have a wooden gallows made,
But hang me on a tree."

"If this be true," Lord Arnold said
"That you have told to me,
I have an estate in Northumberland
Which thy reward shall be." [1]

Lord Arnold he summoned his merry men all,
By ones, by twos and by threes,
He ordered them not a drum should be beat,
Nor a bugle sounded be.

But there was one of Lord Arnold's men
Who loved his lady well,
He raised his bugle to his lips
And he sounded it loud and shrill.

"Hark, O hark!" said Mottha Grow,
"What's that I think I hear?
Methinks I hear Lord Arnold's bugle horn,
A-sounding in my ear.

"And ever as the bugle blows
It seems to me to say,
'Arise and dress ere its too late,
And away, Mottha Grow, away.' " [1]

Lie still, lie still, my Mottha Grow,
And keep me from the cold,
It is nothing but a shepherd boy
A-driving his sheep to the fold."

Lord Arnold he strode through the castle halls
And opened the door so wide.
They did not know Lord Arnold had come
Till he stood by their bedside.

"How do you like my bed," Lord Arnold said,
"And how do you like my sheets,
And how do you like my lady so fair
Who lies at your side so sweet."

"I like your bed very much," said he,
"I also like your sheets,
But much better do I like Lady Arnold so fair,
Who lies at my side so sweet." [1]

"Arise, arise, you Mottha Grow,
And put your clothing on,
For I'll never have it said in Old England
That I slew a naked man."

"Must I arise?" said Mottha Grow,
"And fight you for my life,
While you have a glittering sword by your side
And I have not a knife?"

"Yes, I have a sword here at my side
And others in their place.
You shall have the best one of them
And I will take the worst.

"And you shall have the first full blow,
And strike it like a man.
I will have the next full blow
And I'll kill you if I can."

Mottha Grow he had the first full blow.
It wounded Lord Arnold sore.
Lord Arnold had the next full blow,
Mottha Grow could strike no more.

Lord Arnold then he looked around,
He look-ed him upon,
Saying, "I have killed the handsomest man
That ever the sun shone on."

Lord Arnold he took his lady by the hand
And sat her on his knee,
Saying, "Which do you like the very best now,
This Mottha Grow or me."

"Very well do I like your cherry cheeks,
Very well do I like your chin,
Better, much better do I like that Mottha Grow
Than Lord Arnold and his whole kin."

Lord Arnold he took his lady by the hand
He led her o'er the plain,
She never spoke another full word,
For he split her head in twain.

Sing on, sing on, ye nightengale,
Sing on, sing on, ye sparrow,
Lord Arnold has slain his wife to-day
And he shall be hung to-morrow.

B

*Sung by Eldin Colsie of Stacyville, Maine, as he has always
known the song.*

H. H. F., *Collector*
July 15, 1941

Incomplete tune. Structure: A B . . . B (4,4,4,4); Rhythm
B; Scale: hexatonic

t.c. G.

For mel. rel. see BES, 154.

Lord Banner

Four and twenty ladies
Were playing at a ball.
Lord Banner's wife was there, too,
The fairest of them all,
And young Magrue from Scotland, too,
As fair as the rising sun.

Lord Banner

Tr. H. E. F. B.

Four and twen-ty la - dies Were play - ing at a ball. Lord Ban-ner's wife was there, too, The

(this part spoken off-key)

fair - est of them all, And young Magrue from Scotland,

too, As fair as the rising sun. Oh, she looked at him and he winked at her, And the like, it was nev - er done.

Oh, she looked at him and he winked at her
And the like, it was never done.

Saying, "How would you like to ride with me?"
Saying, "How would you like to ride?
You will have servants to wait upon you
And a fair lady by your side."
"For me to take a ride with you,
I dare not for all my life,
For by the ring upon your finger
You are Lord Banner's wife."

"Oh, what if I am Lord Banner's wife?
Lord Banner is not at home.
He's gone away to Redemption;
He's taking King Henry's throne."
Oh, one of his foot-pages standing by

Who heard all was said and done,
Saying, "Master, he will hear of this
Before the rising sun."

So he ran till he came to the riverside
And he plunged in and he swam.
He swam till he came to the other side
And he took to his heels and he ran.
Oh, he ran till he came to Lord Banner's door
And he knocked about in vim
But no one there was so ready
To let his foot-page in.

"Oh, are there any of my towers down
Or any of my castles three
Or has there anything happened
Unto my gay ladee?"
"Oh, no, there's none of your towers down
Or none of your castles three
But young Magrue from Scotland, too,
Is in bed with your gay ladee."

"If this be a lie you tell to me
As I suppose would be,
I will have a gallows rigged
And it's hanged you shall be."
"If this be a lie I tell to you
As you suppose 'twould be,
You need not have a gallus rigged.
You can hang me on a tree."

Lord Banner called his men all down
By one and by two and by three,
Saying, "Let us ride to fair Scotland
Some fancy for to see."
They put the bugle to their mouths
And they blew both loud and long,

And at the turning of every tune
It was, "Young Magrue, do begone."

"Oh, what is that I hear," said he,
"That sounds so loud and clear?
I think it is Lord Banner's
Bugle that I hear."
"Oh, lay down, lay down. Pray keep me warm.
Pray keep me from the cold.
It is Lord Banner's shepherd.
He's calling the sheep to the fold."

So they both lay down in their pillows warm
And soon fell fast asleep.
It was early the next morning
Lord Banner stood at their feet,
Saying, "How do you like my blankets warm?
Oh, how do you like my sheets
And how do you like my false ladee
Who lies in your arms and sleeps?"

"Right well do I like your blankets warm
And right well do I like your sheets
But better than all your false ladee
Who lies in my arms and sleeps."
"Rise up, rise up and put on your clothes
As quick as ever you can
For never to say in fair Scotland
I fought with a bare naked man."

"For me to rise up and put on my clothes,
I dare not for all my life
For by your side are two glittering swords
And I, not a single knife."
"If by my side are two glittering swords,
They cost me deep in purse.

It's you can have the very best one
And I will take the worst.

"And you can strike the very first blow
And strike it like a man
And I will strike the second one
And I'll kill you if I can."
So young Magrue struck the very first blow.
It wounded Lord Banner sore.
Lord Banner struck the second one
And he laid him in his gore.

Caught his fair lady by the waist
And he gave her kisses three,
Saying, "Now which one do you like the best—
The slain Magrue or me?"
"Right well do I like your rosy cheeks,
Right well your dimpled chin,
But better than all, the slain Magrue
Than you and all of your kin."

He caught her by the hair of the head
And he split her brains in twain.
He threw her down upon the floor
And she never arose again.
The tail of the sword down on the floor
And the point of it to his breast.
There was never three lovers
So quickly sent to rest.

C

Sung by Mrs. Roy Blanchard of Vanceboro, Maine, as known to her Scotch forebears. Printed in the Bangor, Maine, **Daily News,** *December, 30, 1933.*

Mrs. Fannie Eckstorm, Collector
December 30, 1933

Lord Banner's Wife

Four and twenty ladies
Being at a ball,
Lord Banner's wife a-being there,
The flower of them all.

And Young MacGrew from fair Scotland,
As fair as the raising sun,
She looked on him and he looked on her,
The likes were never known.

Saying, "Will you take a ride with me,
O, will you take a ride?
And you shall have servants to wait on you
And a Lady by your side."

"O, no, I dare not ride with you,
No, not for all my life,
For the ring you have on your finger
You are Lord Banner's wife."

"And what if I am Lord Banner's wife?
Lord Banner is not at home.
He has gone to Redemption
To serve King Henry's throne."

Just then one of Lord Banner's merry men
Heard what they said and done.
He said, "I mean Lord Banner shall know
Before the raising sun."

He ran down to the river side
And he jumped in and swam.
He swam till he came to the other side,
Then took to his heels and ran.

He ran till he came to the castle door,
He knocked so long and shrill

There was no one there so eager as
Lord Banner to let him in.

Saying, "Are there any of my castles down,
Or any of my towers three,
Or is my lady brought to bed
With a daughter or a son?"

"Ah, no, there are none of the castles down,
Or none of your towers three,
By (but) Young MacGrew from fair Scotland
Is in bed with your fair Lady."

"Now, if this be a lie
As I suppose it to be,
I will not rig any gallows,
But hang you to a tree."

"And now if this be a lie,
As you suppose it to be,
You need not rig any gallows
But hang me to a tree."

Then Lord Banner called to his merry men
By ones, by twos, by threes.
Saying, "We'll ride to fair Scotland
This couple for to see."

But there was one of Lord Banner's merry men
Who loved his Lady well;
He raised his bugle to his lips
And sounded it loud and shrill.

"Hark, what music is that that I dost hear,
That sounds so loud and shrill?
I believe it's Lord Banner's bugle horn:
If it is I shall come to my end."

"Lie down, lie down and keep me warm,
And keep me from the cold;
'Tis only Lord Banner's shepherd boy
A-calling the sheep to fold."

They huddled, they cuddled,
Till they were fast asleep;
Early the next morning
Lord Banner stood at their feet.

Saying, "How do you like my blankets fine,
And how do you like my sheets,
And how do you like my fair lady
That lies in your arms asleep?"

"It's well I like your blankets fine,
And well I like your sheets,
But better I like your fair Lady
That lies in my arms asleep."

"Arise, arise and put on your clothes
As quick as ever you can;
For I'll never have it said in fair Scotland
I fought with a naked man."

"O, no, I dare not get out of bed,
No, not for all of my life;
For you have sharp swords and sheafs
And I not a single knife."

"Well, what if I have sharp swords and sheafs,
They cost me deep in purse,
But you can have the very best one
And I will take the worst.

"And you will strike the very first blow
And strike it like a man,
And I will strike the second blow
And kill you if I can."

MacGrew he struck the very first blow
And struck Lord Banner full sore;
Lord Banner struck the second blow
And killed him in his gore.

He ran back to the bedside
Where lay his fair Lady,
Saying, "Which one do you like the best,
Young MacGrew or me?"

"It's well I like your rosy cheeks,
It's well I like your hair
But better I liked young MacGrew,
For he is twice as fair."

He grabbed her by the hair of the head
And dragged her onto the floor,
He cut her head from her shoulders.
She never spoke any more.

And then he took the point of the sword
And pointed to his breast,
Saying, "There never were three lovers
Went to a more peaceful rest.

"Go, dig me a grave; go dig me a grave;
Go dig it both long, wide, and deep,
And place my Lady by my side
And Young MacGrew at my feet."

D

Sung by Arthur Walker of Littleton, Maine.

M. Olney, Collector
September 1, 1942

Structure: A B (4,4); Rhythm B; Contour: inverted arc;
Scale: major

t.c. G.

For mel. rel. see BES, 154.

Lord Banner

Tr. M. O.

Four and twen-ty gay la-dies Was
danc-ing at a ball, Lord Ban-ner's wife, Oh,
she was there, The gay-est of them all.

Lord Banner

Four and twenty gay ladies
Was dancing at a ball.
Lord Banner's wife, oh, she was there,
The gayest of them all.

And Young Magrue from Scotland, too,
He being at that ball,
She looked at him, and he winked at her;
The like was never saw.

"Oh, will you take a walk with me,
Or will you take a ride,

Or will you come to my chamber
And lay down by my side?"

"Oh, to take a walk with you
I dare not for my life,
For by the rings on your finger,
You are Lord Banner's wife."

"Oh, what if I am Lord Banner's wife,
Lord Banner's not at home;
He's gone over to old England
For to take in King Henery's throne."

Oh, some of his pages being there
And seeing what was done,
He said, "My master shall hear of this
Before the rise of the sun."

He ran till he came to the river banks;
There he jumped in and he swam.
He swam till he came to the other side;
He took to his heels and ran.

It's when he got to Lord Banner's hall,
He knocked both loud and shrill.
There seemed to be nobody ready
To let his foot-page in.

"Oh, is there any of my castles down,
Or any of my towers three,
Or is there anything has happened
Unto my gay ladye?"

"Oh, no, there's none of your castles down,
And none of your towers three
But young Magrue from Scotland, he
Is in bed with your gay ladye."

"If this is a lie you tell to me,
As I suppose it to be,

For I shall build a gallers high
And hanged on it you will be."

"If this is a lie that I tell to you,
As you suppose it to be,
You need not build a gallers high;
You can hang me to a tree."

He called his arm-ed men out,
By one, by two, and by three,
Saying, "We'll go over to old Scotland;
I'm anxious to see what's happened to my gay ladye."

They put their bugles to their lips,
They played as they marched along,
And at the turn of every tune,
It was "Young Magrue to be gone."

"Oh, what is that that I do hear,
That's ringing in my ears?"
"Lay down, lay down, and keep me warm,
And shield me from the cold.[1]
That is Lord Banner's shepherd boy
Driving his sheep to the fold."

They huddled down, they cuddled down,
They soon fell fast asleep,
And early the next morning
Lord Banner stood there at their feet.

"Oh, how do you like my blankets warm,
And how do you like my sheet?
And how do you like my gay lady
Who lays in your arms and sleeps?"

"Very well I like your blankets warm,
Very well I like your sheet,

[1] Lines 3 and 4 are sung to the same air as lines 1 and 2.

Much better I like that young lady
Than you or any of your kin."

"Git up, git up, and put on your clothes,
As quickly as ever you can;
It will never be said in old Scotland that
I have fought with a naked man."

"Oh, to get up and put on my clothes,
I dare not for my life,
For by your side you have two broadswords,
And I've not a single knife."

"If by my side I have two broadswords,
They've cost me deep in purse.
To you I give the very best one,
And I shall take the worst.

"And you can strike the very first blow,
And strike it like a man;
I will strike the second blow
And I'll kill you if I can."

Oh, young Magrue struck the very first blow,
He wounded Lord Banner sore.
Lord Banner struck the second blow
And he laid Magrue to the floor.

He took his lady by the waist,
He gave her kisses three,
Saying, "Which one of these men do you love the best,
This young Magrue or me?"

"Very well I like your rosy cheeks,
Very well your dimpled chin;
Much better I like that young Magrue
Than you or any of your kin."

He grabbed her by the hair of the head,
He dashed her brains in twain.
He placed the butt of his sword to the floor,

And the point of it to his breast;[1]
And never was three lovyers
That ever went quicker to rest.

E

Sung by Miss Annie Syphers, Monticello, Maine.

M. Olney, Collector
May 8, 1942

Structure: A B A¹ B¹ (8,8,8,8); Rhythm B; Contour: undulating, pendulumlike; Scale: major

t.c. C.

For mel. rel. see BES, 150, 173, 186.

Lord Banner

Tr. M. O.

Four and twen-ty gay la-dies, A-be-ing at a ball, Lord Ban-ner's la-dy, she came there, The gay-est of them all, And John Ma-grue of Scot-land, too, As bright as the ris-ing sun. He looked at her and she winked at him; The likes were nev-er known.

Lord Banner

Four and twenty gay ladies,
A-being at a ball,
Lord Banner's lady, she came there,
The gayest of them all,
And John Magrue of Scotland, too,
As bright as the rising sun,
He looked at her and she winked at him,
The likes were never known.

"Oh, will you take a ride with me,
Oh, will you take a ride?
You shall have servants to wait on you
And a fair lady by your side."
"It's to take a ride, I dare not do it,
Oh, not for all my life,
For by that ring you wear on your finger,
You are Lord Banner's wife."

"Oh, what if I am Lord Banner's wife,
Sure, he is not at home.
He has gone to convention
To take King Henery's throne."
One of his foot-pages being standing by
Heard all was said and done.
He said, "My master shall hear the news
Before the rising sun."

He ran till he came to the river side.
There he jumped in and he swam;
He swam till he came to the other side;
He took to his heels and he run.
He run till he came to the cottage door;
He knocked both loud and shrill.
There's none so ready as Lord Banner
To let his fair page in,

Saying, "Are there any of my castles down,
Or any of my towers three,
Or has there anything happened
To my fair lady?"
"Oh, no, there's none of your castles down,
Nor none of your towers three,
But young Magrue from Scotland's
In bed with your fair lady."

"If this be a lie you tell to me,
As I suppose it to be,
I will rig a gallus
And hanged you shall be."
"If that be a lie I tell to you,
As you suppose it to be,
You need not rig any gallus;
You may hang me on a tree."

He called down his army men
By one, by two, by three,
Saying, "Let us go over to fair Scotland
Our fancies for to see."
"Oh, what is that," said John Magrue,
"That sounds so loud in my ear?
It is Lord Banner's bugle
That sounds so loud and clear."

"Lie down, lie down, and keep me warm,
Pray keep me from the cold.
It is Lord Banner's shepherd boy
A-driving their sheep to the fold."
They huddled and they cuddled,
And they both fell fast asleep,
When early the next morning
Lord Banner stood at their feet,

Saying, "How do you like my blankets fine,
And how do you like our sheets,

And how do you like your false lady
That lies in my arms and sleeps?"
"Full well I like your blankets fine
And well I like your sheets,
But best of all, it's young Magrue
Than you and all o' your kin."

He caught this fair lady by the waist,
He gave her kisses three,
Saying, "Which of us do you like the best,
It's young Magrue or me?"
"Full well I like your rosy cheeks
And well your dimpled chin,
But best of all it's young Magrue
Than you and all of your kin."

He caught her by the hair of the head,
He split her brains in twain.
He threw her on the floor
Where she never rose again.
"Go dig my grave,
Dig it long, wide, and deep,
And place my fair lady by my side
And young Magrue at my feet."

F

*Recorded in Charlestown, New Hampshire, Snumshire
District, from the singing of Orlon Merrill, as learned from
his mother, Mrs. Hattie Main Merrill of Quebec. Printed
in BFSSNE, III, 6. Compare this to G below.*

H. H. F., *Collector*
February 3, 1931

Structure: A^1 A^2 B A^3 (4,4,4,4); Rhythm B; Contour: pendulum; Scale: major

t.c. C.

For mel. rel. see BES, 150, 173, 186.

Lord Banner

Tr. G. B.

Four and twen-ty la-dies fair, all be-ing at a ball, Lord Ban-ner's wife she be-ing there, the fair-est of them all. And Young La-grue from Scot-land as fair as the ris-ing sun, She looked at him and he looked at her, and the like it was nev-er known.

Variants:

Lord Banner

Four and twenty ladies fair, all being at a ball,
Lord Banner's wife, she being there, the fairest of them all,
And Young Lagrue from Scotland as fair as the rising sun,
She looked at him and he looked at her, and the like it was
    never known.

Says she, "Oh, will you take a ride, oh, will you take a ride?
You shall have servants to wait on you and a fair lady by
    your side."
"Oh, no, oh, no, I dare not do it, I'll not, for all of my life,
For by the ring on your forefinger you are Lord Banner's
    wife."

"What if I am Lord Banner's wife: Lord Banner is not at
    home;
He has gone over to Convention to take Young Henry's
    throne."
But one of his pages being there, which heard and see all
    that was done,
He swore that his master should hear of this before the next
    rising sun.

He ran till he came to the river's side and he ploughed to
    his breast and swam;
He swam till he came to the other side and he took to his
    heels and run.
He ran till he came to the castle there; so loud he rapped
    at the door;
And who was there so ready as Lord Banner to let him in.

"Oh, is there any of my towers down nor any of my towers
    three,
Or has there anything happened unto my fair lady?"
"Oh, no, there's none of your towers down, and there's
    none of your towers three

But Young Lagrue from Scotland is in bed with your fair
    lady."

"If this be a lie you tell to me, which I suppose it to be,
I will rig a gallows and hang-ed you shall be."
"If this be a lie I tell to you, which you suppose it to be,
You need not rig a gallows, but hang me on a tree!"

And he called by one of his merry, merry men, by one, by
    two, by three,
Saying, "We will ride over to old Scotland this fair couple
    for to see."
"What's this I hear so loud in my ear that sounds so loud
    and drear?
It is Lord Banner's bugle, and he will soon be here!"

"Lie still, lie still and keep me warm and keep me from the
    cold—
It's only Lord Banner's shepherd boy a-driving the sheep
    to the fold."
They huddled and they cuddled; they both fell fast asleep,
And when they awoke in the morning, Lord Banner, he
    stood at their feet.

"How do you like my blankets fine, and how do you like
    my sheets?
And how do you like that fair maid that lies in your arms
    asleep?"
"Quite well I like your blankets fine, quite well I like your
    sheets,
But I like this fair maid better that lies in my arms asleep."

"Rise up, rise up, put on your clothes as quick as ever you
    can;
I'll never have it said in old Scotland that I fought with a
    naked man
"Oh, no, oh, no, I dare not do it, oh, not for all of my life,

For by your side you have two broadswords while I have
    nary a knife."

"What if I have the two broadswords—they cost me deep
    in purse!
You shall have the very best one, and I will take the worst,
And you may strike the very first blow and strike it like a
    man,
And I will strike the second blow and I'll kill you if I can."

Young Lagrue he struck the very first blow, that wounded
    Lord Banner sore;
Lord Banner struck the second blow and laid him in his
    gore.
Then he took his fair lady by the lily-white hand and he
    gave her kisses three,
Saying, "Which of the two do you love best: this Young
    Lagrue or me?'

"Quite well I like your rosy cheeks, quite well I like your
    chin,
But I'd ten times rather have Young Lagrue than you or
    all of your kin!"
He grabbed her by the hair of the head and he split her
    head in two;
She sank upon her bended knees by the side of Young
    Lagrue.

Then he put the heel of the sword to the floor and the
    point unto his breast,
Saying, "Was there ever three lovers more easily laid at
    rest?
Go dig my grave, go dig my grave, go dig it both wide and
    deep,
And place my fair lady by my side and Young Lagrue at my
    feet."

G

*Mrs. Grant Coville, sister to Orlon Merrill of Charlestown,
New Hampshire, gave this song in her home at Pittsburg,
New Hampshire. Her tune was the same as Mr. Merrill's.
Compare this to F above.*

H. H. F., Collector
June 3, 1941

Lord Banner

Four and twenty ladies fair, all being at a ball,
Lord Banner's wife she being there, the fairest of them all,
And young LaGrue from Scotland, as fair as the rising sun,
She looked at him and he looked at her; the like it was
    never known.

Says she, "Oh, will you take a ride, oh, will you take a ride?
You shall have servants to wait on you and a fair lady by
    your side."
"Oh, no, oh, no, I dare not do it, no, not for all of my life,
For by your ring on your forefinger you are Lord Banner's
    wife."

'Oh, what if I am Lord Banner's wife? Lord Banner is not
    at home.
He is gone over to Condemption to take young Henry's
    throne."
One of his pages being there which heard and see all that
    was done
And swore that his master should hear of this before the
    next rising sun.

He ran till he came to the river shore and he took to his
    heels and he swam.
He swam till he came to the other side and he took to his
    heels and he ran.

He ran till he came to the castle there. So loudly he rapped
  at the door
And who should be there so ready as Lord Banner to let
  him in.

"Oh, is there any of my towers down or any of my towers
  free,
Or has there anything happened unto my fair ladee?"
"Oh, no, there is none of your towers down or none of
  of your towers free
But young LaGrue from Scotland is in bed with your fair
  ladee."

"If this be a lie which you tell to me, which I suppose it
  to be,
I will rig a gallows and hang-ed you shall be."
"If this be a lie which I tell to you, which you suppose it
  to be,
You need not rig a gallows but hang me on a tree."

He called to one of his merry, merry men by one, by two,
  by three,
Saying, "We will go over to old Scotland this fair couple
  for to see."

.   .   .   .

.   .   .   .

"What's this I hear so loud in my ear which sounds so loud
  and drear?
It is Lord Banner's shepherd boy and he will soon be here."
"Lie still, lie still and keep me warm and keep me from the
  cold.
It's only Lord Banner's shepherd boy a-driving the sheep to
  the fold."

They huddled and they cuddled till both fell fast asleep
And when they awoke in the morning Lord Banner he
  stood at their feet.

"Rise up, rise up, put on your clothes as quick as ever you
can.
I never had it said in all Scotland that I fought with a naked
man."

"Oh, no, oh, no, I dare not do it, no, not for all of my life
For by your side you have two broadswords while I have nary
a knife."
"What if I have two broadswords? They cost me deep in
purse.
You may have the very best one and I will take the worst,

"And you may strike the very first blow and strike it like a
man
And I will strike the second blow and I will kill you if I
can."
So young LaGrue he struck the very first blow which
wounded Lord Banner sore.
Lord Banner he struck the second blow and laid him in his
gore.

He took his lady by the lily-white hand and he gave her
kisses three,
Saying, "Which of the two do you love best, young LaGrue
or me?"
"Quite well I like your red rosy cheeks, quite well I like
your chin,
But I ten times rather have young LaGrue or you or all of
your kin."

He grabbed her by the hair of her head and split her head
in two.
She sank down upon her bended knees by the side of young
LaGrue.
Then he put the heel of his sword to the floor and the point
unto his breast,

Saying, "Was there ever three lovers more easily laid at
    rest?"

H

*Sung by Hanford Hayes in Stacyville, Maine, to H. H. F.
and A. C. B.*

H. H. F., Collector
September 22, 1940

Lord Banner

Four and twenty ladies
Assembled at a ball,
Lord Banner's wife she being there,
The fairest of them all,
And young MaGrew from Scotland
As fair as any king.
He looked at her and she winked at him—
The like was never known.

"Or will you take a sleighride,
Or will you take a walk?
You shall have servants to wait on you
And a fair lady by your side."
"I dare not take a sleighride,
No, not for all my life,
For by the ring that you wear on your finger,
You are Lord Banner's wife."

"What if I am Lord Banner's wife?
I hear he's not to home.
He has gone over to Scotland to
Receive young Henry's throne."
The servant boy, he listening
To all that was said and done,
He swore he'd tell his master
Before the rising sun.

He ran till he came to the river's side;
He jumped in and he swum;
And when he got to the other shore,
He took to his heels and he run.
"Is any of my castles down
Or any of my towers three
Or is there anything wrong with
My own, my fair ladee?"

"No, there's none of your castles down
Or none of your towers three,
But young MaGrew from Scotland, too,
Is in bed with your fair ladee."
"If this be a lie that you tell to me,
As I suppose it to be,
Then I shall rig a gallows
And hang-ed you shall be."

"If this be a lie that I tell to you,
As you suppose it to be,
You need not rig any gallows
But hang me to a tree."
He call-ed all his soldiers,
By one, by two and by three,
Saying, "We'll go over to Scotland,
Our fancies for to see."

"Oh, how do you like my bed, sir,
And how do you like my sheets
And how do you like my false ladee
Who lies in your arms and sleeps?"
"Oh, well I like your blankets, sir,
Oh, well I like your sheets
But better I like your false ladee
Who lies in my arms asleep."

"Rise up, rise up, young Matt MaGrew,
Rise up as quick as you can,

For it never shall be said in fair Scotland
I killed a naked man."
"Oh, to rise up I dare not do;
Oh, not for all of my life,
For by your side hangs two broadswords
And I, not a single knife."

"If by my side hangs two broadswords
And you not a single knife,[1]
And you shall take the better one
And I shall take the worst.
And you may have the very first blow
And strike it like a man
And I will have the second blow
And kill you if I can."

Young MaGrew had the very first blow
And wounded Lord Banner sore,
And Lord Banner had the second blow
And left him in his gore.
He caught his fair lady by the waist;
He gave her kisses three,
Saying, "Which of us do you like the best,
Your young MaGrew or me?"

"Oh, well I like your rosy cheeks,
Likewise your dimpled chin,
But better I like my young MaGrew
Than you or all of your kin."
He caught her by the hair of the head
And he split her head in twain.
He threw her body on the floor
And it never rose again.

He put the hilt of his sword to the floor,
The point of it to his breast,

[1] On December 7, 1940, Mr. Hayes returned to H. H. F. a typed copy
she had sent him of his September singing with this line corrected as
follows:

They cost me deep in price

Saying, "Was there ever two true lovers met
So quickly sent to rest?"

1

*Sung by Charles Finnemore of Bridgewater, Maine, as he
learned it from his sister.*

M. Olney, Collector
October 28, 1943

Structure: A B C D♭ (4,4,4,4); Rhythm B; Contour: undulating; Scale: major

t.c. B-flat.

For mel. rel. see BES, 186 (not close).

Lord Banner

Tr. H. E. F. B.

Lord Banner

There's four and twenty ladies
All gathered at a ball,
Lord Banner's wife she being there,
The fairest one of all,
And Young Magrue from Scotland, too,
Fair as the rising sun.
He looked at her, she winked at him,
The likes was never known.

"Nor would you take a walk with me,
Or would you take a ride?
There's men and maid-servants to wait upon you
And a fair lady by your side."
"For me to take a ride with you,
I dare not on my life,
For by the ring on your finger,
You are Lord Banner's wife."

"Now, what if I be Lord Banner's wife?
Oh, he is not at home.
He is over in Scotland,
A-visitin' Lord Henery's home."
The little page being standing by,
He heard what they had said and done.
He says, "My master shall hear the news
Before the rising sun."

He ran till he came to the river side,
Then he jumped in and swum.
He swam till he came to the other side,
He took to his heels and run.
He ran till he come to Lord Banner's hall,
So loudly he did ring,

There was none so ready as Lord Banner himself
To rise and let him in.

"Oh, is any of my temples down,
Or any of my castles three
Or is there anything the matter
With my fair ladye?"
"No, there is none of your castles down,
Nor none of your palaces three,
But Young Magrue from Scotland
Lies with your fair ladye."
"If this be true you tell to me,
A rich man you shall be."
"If this be false I tell to you,
I'll be hanged on the gallus tree."

J

*As sung by Mrs. Phyllis MacDonald Burditt of Springfield,
Vermont, who learned it from her father, William
MacDonald, who was born in Scotland in 1834. He migrated
to Canada at the age of 12. Printed in* The New Green
Mountain Songster, *135, and in the Springfield, Mass.,*
Republican, *July 26, 1931.*

H. H. F., Collector
June 14, 1931

Structure: A¹ A² (4,4); Rhythm B; Contour: each half an
arc; Scale: major

t.c. B-flat.

For mel. rel. see BES, 173; BF, 78, top of page.

Lord Banner

Tr. M. O.

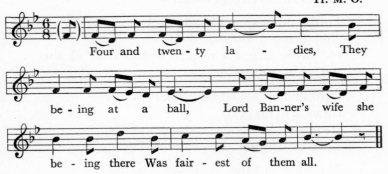

Four and twen - ty la - dies, They be - ing at a ball, Lord Ban-ner's wife she be - ing there Was fair - est of them all.

Lord Banner

Four and twenty ladies,
They being at a ball,
Lord Banner's wife, she being there
Was fairest of them all,

And Young LaGrove from Scotland
As fair as the rising sun.
He looked at her, she looked at him,
And then their love begun.

"Oh, won't you take a ride," said she,
"Oh, won't you take a ride?
And you shall have servants to wait on you
And a fair lady by your side."

"No, no, I'll not take a ride," said he,
"Not on my very life
For the ring that you wear on your finger now
Makes you Lord Banner's wife."

"Well, what if I am Lord Banner's wife?
Lord Banner is not at home.

He has gone to the London Convention for
To seat King George on his throne."

Lord Banner's valet hearing this
And seeing all that was done,
He swore that his master should hear of this
Before the next rising sun.

Lord Banner's valet knowing this,
He took to his heels and ran;
He ran till he came to the water's edge
Then he breasted the stream and swam.

And when he came to the castle walls,
How fiercely the bells did ring;
There was no one so eager as Lord Banner
To arise and let him in,

Saying, "Are any of my castles over
Or any of my towers down
Or has my fair lady been taken ill
Since I have left the town?"

"There are none of your castles over—
I swear it by my life—
But Young LaGrove from Scotland
Is making love to your wife."

"If this be a lie that you tell to me—
As I suppose it to be,
I will erect a gallows high
And hang-ed you shall be."

"If this be a lie that I tell to you,
As you suppose it to be,
You need not erect a gallows high
But may hang me to a tree."

Lord Banner then called up his martial men;
He called them one, two and three,

Saying, "Come, we'll ride over to Scotland
This happy couple to see."

"Oh, what is that? Oh, what is that?
It fills my soul with fear,
I fear 'tis Lord Banner's bugle call.
I fear he is drawing near."

"Lie down, lie down and keep me warm
And keep me from the cold.
'Tis only Lord Banner's shepherd boy
Calling his sheep to fold."

They huddled and they cuddled
And they soon fell fast asleep
And when they awoke in the morning
Lord Banner stood at their feet,

Saying, "How do you like my blankets fine
And how do you like my sheets
And how do you like my fair young bride
Who lies in your arms asleep?"

"Very well do I like your blankets fine
And well do I like your sheets
But better by far your lady fair
Who lies in my arms asleep."

"Get up, get up and put on your clothes
As fast as ever you can,
For it ne'er shall be said in old Scotland
That I fought with a naked man."

"No, I will not get up and put on my clothes
As fast as ever I can,
For you have two broadswords by your side
While I have my naked hands."

"What if I have got two broadswords.
They are each with pearl inlaid

And you may have your choice of these
For each is a trusty blade.

"And you may strike the very first blow
But strike it like a man
And I will strike the second blow
And I'll kill you if I can."

LaGrove he struck the very first blow
And he wounded Lord Banner full sore.
Lord Banner struck the second blow
And he laid him in his gore.

He took his fair lady by the hand
And he gave her kisses three
Saying, "Why do you love this young LaGrove
So much better than you do me?"

"Very well do I like your ruby lips,
Very well do I like your chin
But better I love this young LaGrove
Than you or any of your kin."

He took her by her long yellow hair
And he cleft her head in twain.
Lady Banner fell upon her knees
Never to rise again.

"Go dig my grave," Lord Banner cried,
"And dig it broad and deep
And lay my fair lady by my side
And Young LaGrove at our feet."

Lord Banner then fell upon his sword
After giving his love one last kiss.
Have you ever heard of three lovers dying
So tragic a death as this?

When this song was sung by Mrs. Burditt, her husband, El-
win Burditt, added:

"I will not get up and put on my clothes
As quick as ever I can
For wouldn't I be a fool indeed to fight
An armed and angry man?"

Child Maurice

(Child 83)

This ballad is no longer sung in England or America and, at best, is very rare in Scotland where it was so well-known during the eighteenth century. In 1755 a text, re-published in Glasgow from an earlier edition, had wide distribution, and in 1756 John Home used the plot of the song for his tragedy, *Douglas*. The popularity of the play increased the already considerable vogue of the ballad and printed texts passed into oral tradition to affect the older versions already in existence there.

In America, Elisabeth B. Greenleaf and Grace Y. Mansfield, *Ballads and Sea Songs of Newfoundland* (Cambridge, Mass., 1924), 25, give an abbreviated and recited text with a "Gil Morissy" title. The *Charms of Melody* version, of course, was copied from a ballad book. It is almost exactly like a text printed in Greig and Keith, 64-67. It includes 47½ of the 48 stanzas, and even the dialect is much the same. It differs mainly in the name of the hero, which is Child Maurice rather than Gill Morice. The Greig text is sung by Ewan MacColl on Riverside Records, RLP 12-625 (*The English and Scottish Popular Ballads*, Volume 3, Side 2). Child, II, 263 f., is useful in studying the history of this song, but there is little bibliography to give.

Copied literatim et punctatim by H. H. F. from a compilation of 400 pages of numbered issues of The Charms of

Melody: *or* Siren Medley, *printed by J. & J. Carrick,*
Bachelor's Walk, Dublin. The watermark on the title page
reads GREAT NEWTON, with the date 1818. Copies
are available at the Boston Athenaeum; the John Hay Li-
brary at Brown University (60 pages, dated 1824, beginning
with Volume 1, page 1); and at the Library of Congress.

H. H. F., Collector
August 1, 1958

Child Maurice

This is undoubtedly the true title of this incomparable
Ballad though corrupted into Gil Morrice by the nurfes and
old women, from whofe mouths it was originally published
—Child feems to have been applicable to a young nobleman
when about the age of fifteen. It occurs in Shakefpear's Lear,
in the following line, probably borrowed from fome old romance or ballad.

"Child Roland to the dark tower came."——
Act III—Scene VII.

CHILD Maurice was an earl's fon,
  His name it waxed wide;
It was not for his riches great,
  Nor yet his mickle pride,
But it was for his mother gay
  Who liv'd on Carron fide.

"Where fhall I get a bonny boy
  "That will win hofe and fhoen,
"That will go to Lord Bernard's hall,
  "And bid his lady come?

"And he may run errand, Willie,
  "And he may run with fpeed;
"When other boys go on their feet
  "Ye fhall have prancing fteed."

"Oh, no! oh, no! my mafter dear!
  "I dare not for my life;
"I'll not go to the bold baron's,
  "For t'entice forth his wife."

"My bird Willie, my boy Willie,
  "My dear, Willie" he faid,
"How can you ftrive againft the ftream?
  "For I muft be obeyed."

"But, oh, my mafter dear," he cry'd,
  "In Greenwood ye're your lane;
"Give o'er fuch thoughts I wad ye rid,
  "For fear ye fhould be ta'en."

"Hafte, hafte, I fay, go to the hall,
  "Bid her come here with fpeed;
"If ye refufe my high command,
  "I'll make your body bleed.

"Go, bid her take this gay mantel,
  " 'Tis a' gowd but the hem:
Bid her come to the good Greenwood,
  "E'en by herfelf alane:

"And there it is, a filken fcarfe,
  "Her own hand few'd the fleeve;
"And bid her come to Child Maurice;
  "Afk no bold baron's leave."

"Yes, I will go your black errand,
  "Though it be to your coft;
"Since ye will not be warn'd by me,
  "In it ye will find froft.

"The baron he's a man of might,
  "He ne'er could bide to taunt;
"And ye will fee before 'tis night,
  "Small caufe you have to vaunt.

"And fine I may your errand run,
   "So fore againft my will,
"I'll make a vow, and keep it too,
   "It fhall be done for ill."

When he came to the broken bridge,
   He bent his bow and fwam;
And when he came to grafs growing,
   Set down his feet and ran.

And when he came to Bernard's gate,
   Would neither rap nor call,
But fet his bent bow to his breaft,
   And lighty leap'd the wall.

He would not tell the man his errand
   Though he ftood at the gate;
But ftraight into the hall he came,
   Where they were fet at meat.

"Hail! hail! my gentle fire, and dame!
   "My meffage will not wait,
"Dame, you maun to the Greenwood go,
   "Before it be too late.

"You're bid to take this gay mantel,
   " 'Tis a 'gowd but the hem:
"You maun hafte to the good Greenwood,
   "E'en by yourfelf alone.

"And there it is, a filken fcarfe,
   "Your own hand few'd the fleeve;
"You maun go fpeak to Child Maurice;
   "Afk no bold baron's leave.

The lady ftamped with her foot,
   And winked with her eye;
But all that fhe could fay or do,
   Forbid he would not be.

"It's furely to my bower-woman,
  "It ne'er could be to me."
"I brought it to lord Bernard's lady;
  "I thought that you be fhe."

Then up and fpeak the wily nurfe,
  (The bairn upon her knee)
"If it become from Child Maurice,
  "It's dear welcome to me."

"Ye lie, ye lie, thou filthy nurfe,
  "So loud as I heir you lie;
"I brought it to lord Bernard's lady,
  "I'm fure you are not fhe."

Then up and fpeak the bold baron,
  An angry man was he;
He's tane the table with his foot,
  So has he with his knee,
Till chryftal cup and azar difh
  In flinders he made flie.

"Go bring a robe of your cliding,
  "With all the hafte you can,
"And I'll go to the good Greenwood,
  "And fpeak with your lemman."

"Oh, bide at home now lord Bernard!
  "I warn you bide at home;
"Ne'er wyte a man for violence,
  "Who ne'er wyte you with none."

Child Maurice fat in the Greenwood,
  He wiftled and he fung;
"Oh, what means all the folk coming?
  "My mother tarries long."

The baron to the Greenwood came,
  With mickle dule and care;

And there he firft fpy'd Child Maurice,
   Combing his yellow hair.

"No wonder, no wonder, Child Maurice,
   "My lady loves thee weel:
"The faireft part of my body
   "Is blacker than thy heil.

"Yet ne'er the lefs now, Child Maurice,
   "For all thy great beauty,
"You'll rue the day you ere was born;
   "That head fhall go with me."

Now he has drawn his trufty brand,
   And flaided owr the ftrae;
And through Child Maurice' fair body
   He gar'd the cold iron gae.

And then he took Child Maurice' head,
   And fet it on a fpear;
The meaneft man in all his train,
   Has gotten that head to bear.

And he has tane Child Maurice up,
   Laid him acrofs his fteed;
And brought him to his painted bower,
   And laid him on a bed.

The lady on the caftle wall,
   Beheld both dale and down;
And there fhe faw Child Maurice' head
   Come trailing to the town.

"Better I love that bloody head,
   "Bot and that yellow hair,
"Than lord Bernard and all his lands,
   "As they lie here and there."

And fhe has tane Child Maurice' head,
  And kifs'd both cheek and chin;
"I was once fond of Child Maurice,
  "As the hip is of the ftane.

"I got you in my father's houfe
  "With mickle fin and fhame;
"I brought ye up in the Greenwood,
  "Known to myfelf alane:

"Oft have I by thy cradle fat,
  "And fondly feen thee fleep;
"But now I may go 'bout thy grave
  "A mother's tears to weep."

Again fhe kifs'd his bloody cheek,
  Again his bloody chin;
"Better I lov'd my fon Maurice,
  "Than all my kiff and kin!"

"Away, away, ye ill woman,
  "An ill death may you die!
"If I had known he was your fon,
  "He ne'er been flain by me"

"Upbraid me not, my lord Bernard!
  "Upbraid me not for fhame!
"With that fame fpear, oh, pierce my heart,
  "And fave me from my pain!

"Since nothing but Child Maurice' head
  "Thy jealous rage could quell,
"Let that fame hand now take her life,
  "That ne'er to thee done ill.

"To me no after days nor nights
  "Will ere be fafe or kind:
"I'll fill the air with heavy fighs
  "And greet till I be blind.

"Enough of blood by me's been fpilt,
   "Seek not your death from me;
"I'd rather it had been myfelf,
   "Than either him or thee.

"With hopelefs woe I hear your plaint,
   "Sore, fore I rue the deed—
"That ere this curfed hand of mine
   "Should make his body bleed!

"Dry up your tears, my winfome dame,
   "They ne'er can hail the wound;
"You fee his head upon the fpear,
   "His heart's blood on the ground.

"I curfe the hand that did the deed,
   "The heart that thought the ill,
"The feet that bore me with fuch fpeed,
   "The comely youth to kill.

"I'll e're lament for Child Maurice
   "As if he were my ane;
"I'll ne'er forget the dreary day
   "On which the youth was flain."

Barbara Allen

(Child 84)

In America, "Barbara Allen" has the widest geographical spread and overall currency of any ballad. It is not quite so popular in Britain, in spite of the well-known comments by Samuel Pepys and Oliver Goldsmith concerning its excellence. Nor are there Western or Northern European analogues, although a Spanish romance treats the same theme (certainly not a unique one) and a Serbian song (*see WF,* VIII, 371) is strikingly similar. The ultimate source of the Anglo-American texts has never been located, nor has James Graeme, the hero of the Scottish tradition, been identified.

"Barbara Allen" has a tradition in print, on broadsheets, in song books, on the stage, that is particularly vigorous across Britain and America. As a result, the plot of the spiteful girl and the unhappy lover is much the same wherever the song is found. Nevertheless, all sorts of minor variations have crept into the texts. The ballad may open in the spring or at Martinmas; the lover's name may be William, James, David, etc., etc.; he may give Barbara gifts as he dies; he may curse her; she may curse him; she may blame her parents for the whole mess; and so forth. Frequently, at least in this country, the song ends with a cliché: the "rose and briar" stanza, the "turtle-dove" stanza, or a warning to "ye virgins all." Detailed discussions of the local texts are given by most editors. The best are in Arthur K. Davis' *Traditional Ballads of Virginia* (Cambridge, Mass., 1929), 302-4; in C. A. Smith's treatment of

the song in *Musical Quarterly*, II, 109; and in W. Roy
MacKenzie's *Ballads and Sea-Songs from Nova Scotia* (Cambridge, Mass., 1928), 35. Coffin, 89-90, also gives a list of
interesting variations that have occurred in the American
texts. From such discussions one can see that the "rose-briar"
ending (Flanders E-G), not found in Child, and the references to the tavern toasts in which Barbara was slighted
(most of the Flanders texts) are the characteristic New
World traits.

Flanders A-C follow Child A in the Martinmas opening
and the hero's name. Undoubtedly such texts stem from
the Scottish tradition represented in J. S. Locke's *Forget-
Me-Not Songster*, printed in Boston and known all over the
Northeast. Flanders D f. are of the Child B, a seventeenth-
century broadside, type. This is the most widespread form of
the song. The basin of blood and the gifts offered by the
dying man to Barbara (see Flanders D, F, and G, for example) are not in Child B, though common enough in the
northern American regions. As the song has been frequently localized, it is likely that Flanders E, entitled "Mary
Alling," recalls some nineteenth-century belle. In a similar
way, Flanders O may reflect local events. Phillips Barry,
British Ballads from Maine, 200, notes a tale told around
Newbury, Vermont, about a certain Barbara Allen who was
jilted by her lover in favor of a girl he described as an
"angel without wings." The Flanders H$^{1-3}$ and K$^{1-2}$ series
offer interesting comparisons for the study of ballad variations and transmission. Flanders J, where the lover points
to the basin where he "threw up" his heart's blood, teeters
on comedy. And L, mentioning the Christmas Day Kissing,
is unique.

Any song as popular as "Barbara Allen" will have many
uses. Benjamin A. Botkin, *American Play-Party Song* (Lin-
coln, Nebraska, 1937), 58, cites its development as a game
song. Coffin, 87-88 (American); Dean-Smith, 51, and Belden,

60-61 (English); and Greig and Keith, 67-70 (Scottish) give one a start on an extensive bibliography of texts from oral tradition. See Kittredge's notes in *JAF*, XXIX, 160-61, and XXX, 317, for song book and broadside references. Phillips Barry, *British Ballads from Maine*, 195-200, includes it.

With the exception of the Smith tune, all of the tunes for Child 84 are related. They can be subdivided as follows: 1) Richards, Degreenia, Reynolds; 2) Barlow; 3) Sullivan, Wilson, Armstrong, Halvosa, Fairbanks (which is also related to the Richards group, see end of line 1); 4) Bush; 5) Merrill; and 6) Braid, which is also close to the Sullivan group, at the beginning. Of the great multitude of related tunes, only a selected few, rather closely related ones, are given. Relations are found for groups 1 and 4 to a greater extent than for the others.

A

Mrs. Florence Underhill, with her two sisters, the Misses Young, at Bellows Falls, Vermont, recalled this song, known to their father, Edward O. Young (brother of the late Dr. Ellis of Brookfield, Vermont). Mr. Young had a remarkable memory. His text is close to the version in his Forget-Me-Not Songster, *although it was sung from memory.*

H. H. F., *Collector*
November 2, 1938

Barbara Allen

It fell about the Martimas day
When the green leaves were falling
Sir James the Graham in the west country
Fell in love with Barbara Allen.

She was a fair and comely maid
And a maid nigh to his dwelling

Which made him to admire the more
The beauty of Barbara Allen.

"Oh, what's thy name, my bonny maid;
Oh, where hast thou thy dwelling?"
She answered him most modestly,
"My name is Barbara Allen."

"Oh see you not yon seven ships
So bonny as they are sailing?
I'll make you mistress of them all,
My bonny Barbara Allen."

But it fell out upon a day
At the wine as they were drinking,
They tossed their glasses 'round about
And slighted Barbara Allen.

Oh, she has taken it so ill out
That she'd no more look on him
And for all the letters he could send
Still swore she'd never have him.

"Oh, if I had a man, a man,
A man within my dwelling,
That will write a letter with my blood
And carry it to Barbara Allen.

"Desire her to come here with speed,
For I am at the dying,
And speak one word to her true love
For I'll die for Barbara Allen."

His man is off with all his speed
To the place where she is dwelling.
"Here's a letter from my master dear,
Gin ye be Barbara Allen."

When she looked the letter upon
With a loud laughter gi'ed she;

But ere she read the letter through,
The tear blinded her eye.

Oh, slowly, slowly rose she up
And slowly gaed she to him
And slightly drew the curtains by:
"Young man, I think you're dying."

"Oh, I am sick and very sick,
And my heart is at the breaking.
One kiss or two from thy sweet mouth
Would keep me from the dying."

"Oh, mind you not, young man," said she,
"When you sat in the tavern.
Then you made the health go 'round
And slighted Barbara Allen."

And slowly, slowly rose she up,
And slowly, slowly left him,
And sighing said she could not stay
Since death of life had reft him.

She had not gone a mile from town
Till she heard the death bell knelling
And every knell that death bell gave
Was woe to Barbara Allen.

Now when the virgin heard the same,
Sure, she was greatly troubled;
When in the coffin his corpse she viewed
Her sorrows all were doubled.

"What, hast thou died for me?" she cried,
"Let all true lovers shun me.
Too late I may this sadly say,
That death has quite undone me.

"O mother, mother, make my bed.
Oh, make it soft and narrow.

Since my love died for me today
I'll die for him tomorrow."

B

*This song was known to Mrs. Ella Doten, North Calais,
Vermont, and contributed as she heard it sung when a
child. Copied literatim et punctatim.*

H. H. F., Collector
Summer, 1933

Barbara Allen

It fell about the Martinmas day,
When the green leaves were falling,
Sir James the Graham in the west country,
Fell in love with Barbara Allen.

She was a fair and comely maid,
And a maid nigh to his dwelling
Which made him to admire the more,
The beauty of Barbara Allen.

O what's thy name my bonny maid,
Or where hast thou thy dwelling,
She answer'd him most modestly,
My name is Barbara Allen.

O see you not yon seven ships,
So bonny as they are sailing,
I'll make you mistress of them all,
My bonny Barbara Allen.

But it fell out upon a day,
At the wine as they were drinking,
They toasted their glasses around about,
And slighted Barbara Allen.

O she has taken't so ill ont,
That she'd no more look on him,

And for all the letters he could send,
She swore she'd never have him.

O if I had a man, a man,
A man within my dwelling,
That will write a letter with my blood,
And carry't to Barbara Allen.

Desire her to come here with speed,
For I am at the dying!
And speak one word to her true love,
For I'll die for Barbara Allen.

His man is off with all his speed,
To the place where she is dwelling,
Here's a letter from my master dear,
Gin ye be Barbara Allen.

O when she looked the letter upon,
With a loud laughter gi'd she,
But e'er she read the letter through,
The tear blinded her eye.

O hooly, hooley,[1] rose she up,
And slowly gaed she to him,
And slightly drew the curtains by,
Young man I think you're dying.

O I am sick, and very sick,
And my heart is at the breaking,
One kiss or two of thy sweet mouth,
Would keep me from the dying.

O mind you not young man said she,
When you sat in the tavern,
Then you made the health go round,
And slighted Barbara Allen.

---

[1] "hooly, hooley": "slowly, slowly"

And slowly, slowly, rose she up,
And slowly, slowly, left him,
And sighing said she could not stay,
Since death of life had reft him.

She had not gone a mile from the town,
Till she heard the dead bell knelling,
And every knell that dead bell gave,
Was wo to Barbara Allen.

Now when the virgin heard the same,
Sure she was greatly troubled,
When in the coffin his corpse she view'd,
Her sorrows all were doubled.

What! hast thou died for me, she cried,
Let all true lovers shun me,
Too late I may this sadly say,
That death has quite undone me.

O mother, mother make my bed,
O make it soft and narrow,
Since my love died for me to-day,
I'll die for him to-morrow.

C

*As sung by Mrs. Lily Delorme of Cadyville, New York.
Mrs. Delorme was born in Schuyler Falls, New York, in
1869. Her father was born in Starksboro, Vermont; her
mother, in Schuyler Falls. This ballad was learned in her
childhood home.*

*M. Olney, Collector
December 4, 1941*

Barbara Allen

It was in about Martinmas time,
When the green leaves were a-falling

That Sir John Graham of the North Countries
Fell in love with Barbary Allen.

Now she is taken so ill out,
And she'll no more look on him,
And all the letters he can send,
She still vows she'll never have him.

"Oh, if I had a man, a man,
A man within my dwelling,
To write a letter in my blood,
And carry it to Barbary Allen."

Then slowly, slowly she up,
And slowly, slowly went to him
And softly moved the curtain aside,
Saying, "Young man, I think you're a-dying.

"Mind you not, young man," she said,
"When you were in the tavern a-drinking,
You made the health go 'round and 'round,
And you slighted Barbary Allen."

" 'Tis I am sick and very sick,
And it is for Barbary Allen,
But just one kiss from your sweet lips
Would keep me from a-dying."

Then slowly, slowly raised she up,
And slowly, slowly left him,
And sighing said she could not stay,
Since death of life had reft him.

But ere she got one mile from town,
She heard the death bell knelling,
And every knell that death bell tolled,
Was woe to Barbary Allen.

"O mother, mother, make my bed!
And make it soft and narrow!

Since my love's died for me today,
I will die for him tomorrow."

D

Sung by Mrs. Belle Richards of Colebrook, New Hampshire.

M. Olney, Collector
November 21, 1941

Structure: A B C D (2,2,2,2); **Rhythm** E; **Contour:** arc; **Scale:** major

t.c. G.

For mel. rel. see FCB4, 59(A) (4); EO, 54.

Barbara Allen

Tr. H. E. F. B.

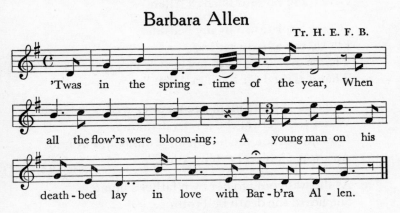

'Twas in the spring-time of the year, When all the flow'rs were bloom-ing; A young man on his death-bed lay in love with Bar-b'ra Al-len.

Barbara Allen

'Twas in the springtime of the year,
When all the flow'rs were blooming,
A young man on his deathbed lay
In love with Barb'ra Allen.

He sent a message to the town
Where this fair maid was dwelling,
Saying, "My master'd like to speak with you
If your name is Barb'ra Allen."

So slowly, slowly rose she up;
So slowly she came riding,
And all she said when she got there
Was, "Young man, I fear you're dying."

"A dying man I am not yet.
One kiss from you would cure me."
"One kiss from me you could not have
If your heart should break with sorrow."

"Go you, look up by my bedside,
For there's a napkin hanging.
There's my gold watch and my gold chain.
Give them both to Barb'ra Allen.

"Go ye, look down by my bedside,
For there's a basin setting
That is overflown with my heart's blood
That was shed for Barb'ra Allen."

Said she, "Young man, I remember well
When you were at the tavern drinking,
How you drank the health all around and 'round
And you slighted Barb'ra Allen."

As she was going to her own father's home,
She heard the death bell tolling,
And in its toll it seemed to roll,
"Hard-hearted Barb'ra Allen."

As she stood in her own father's door,
She saw the hearse a-coming,

Saying, "Come this way with the corpse of clay
That I may gaze upon him."

The more she gazed, the more she scorned,
The more she looked upon him,
The ladies all cried out, "Oh, shame!
Hard-hearted Barb'ra Allen."

"Oh, mother, go and make my bed.
Go make it soft for sorrow.
My true love died for me last night,
And I'll die for him tomorrow.

"Go, father, go and dig my grave.
Go dig it soft and mellow,
And on my grave plant roses red
That I may rest forever."

E

*As sung by Oscar Degreenia in West Cornwall, Connecticut,
to H. H. F. and Mrs. H. S. Beal. His parents sang many
songs to their children—eight of them—when they lived in
a log house at Barton, Vermont. Mr. Degreenia moved to
West Cornwall seventeen years ago. Printed in* Ballads Migrant in New England, *197.*

H. H. F., Collector
May 16, 1949

Structure: A B C D (2,2,2,2); Rhythm B and C but divergent; Contour: arc; Scale: major

t.c. G.

For mel. rel. see FCB4, 59(A) (4).

Mary Alling

Tr. M. O.

Mary Alling

'Twas early in the springtime of the year
When all the flowers were blooming
A young man on his dying bed
In love with Mary Alling.

Slowly she rose, slowly she rose
And slowly she went to him.
When she got there, "Young man," she said,
"I really think you're dying."

"A dying man I am not yet.
One kiss from you would save me."

"One kiss from me you never shall have
If your heart was really a-breaking.

"Do you remember in the dancing hall
When all the music were ringing
You danced around with all the rest
And slighted Mary Alling?

"Do you remember to your father's house
To a place called dwelling
You drank your wine with all the rest
And slighted Mary Alling?"

"You look to the head of my bed;
There is a napkin hanging.
Into it is my gold watch and chain.
It's all for Mary Alling.

"You look to the side of my bed;
There is a basin standing.
It quite overflows with my heart's blood
I shed for Mary Alling."

As she was standing in her father's gate
She heard the church bell tolling
And every time the church bell tolled
It sounded, "Mary Alling."

As she was standing in her father's gate
She saw the hearse a-coming.
"Pull down, pull down that cold, cold corpse,
So I can gaze upon him."

And the more she gazed and the more she scorned
And the more she gazed upon him
Until the girls did all cry out,
"A shame on Mary Alling."

Unto her mother she did go
And unto her did say,
"O mother, mother, make my bed,
Go and make it long and narrow;
My true love died for me today,
I'll die for him tomorrow."

Unto her father she did go
And unto him did say,
"O father, father, dig my grave,
Go and dig it long and narrow;
My true love died for me today,
I'll die for him tomorrow."
And on his grave there grew a rose
And onto hers a briar.
They grew so tall, they grew so tall
And twined away together.

F

Sung by Steven Barlow of Mars Hill, Maine.

M. Olney, Collector
August 30, 1942

Structure: A B C D (2,2,2,2); Rhythm E; Contour: arc;
Scale: major

t.c. B-flat.

Barb'ry Allen

It was early in the spring,
Where all things were blooming,
A young man sick on his dead-bed lay,
For the love of Barb'ry Allen.

Barb'ry Allen

Tr. M. O.

It was ear-ly in the spring, When all things were bloom-ing; A young man sick on his dead-bed lay For the love of Bar-b'ry Al-len.

He sent a message to her home,
The place where she was dwelling;
"There's a message that I send for you,
O dearest Barb'ry Allen."

A-slowly, slowly, she arose,
A-slowly she went to see him,
And when she reached the sick-bed side,
Said, "Young man, you are dying."

"A dying man indeed I am;
A kiss from you will cure me."
"A kiss from me which you'll never have,
If your false heart is breaking.

"Do you remember the other night,
While in your temper of drinking

You drank your ale and your friends and all
In spite of Barb'ry Allen?"

Oh, he turned his pale face to the wall,
He began in saying,
"Adieu, adieu, to my friends and all,
And to my dearest Barb'ry Allen.

"As you stand by my sick-bed side,
You'll see the basin sitting.
It's full of tears and it's all for you,
O dearest Barb'ry Allen.

"As you stand by my sick-bed side,
You'll see the best coat hanging.
Oh, take my watch and chains and my diamond ring;
I'll give them to Barb'ry Allen."

She hasn't gone an hour from town,
She heard the church bell ringing
And in the chime, it seems to say,
"How cruel was Barb'ry Allen."

She hasn't gone an hour from home,
She seen a dead corpse coming.
She begged the crowd for to lay him down
So she could gaze upon him.

"O father, dear, go dig my grave,
Go dig it long and narrow,
For my true love died for me today,
And I'll die for him tomorrow."

So in the churchyard David lay,
And they did lay together,
And in the grave there grew a rose,
And on the rose a briar.

G

Mrs. Ellen M. Sullivan, of Springfield, Vermont, who came as a young child to America in 1867, a native of County Cork, Ireland, sang this version.

H. H. F., Collector
July 12, 1932

Structure: A B C D (2,2,2,2); Rhythm E; Contour: arc; Scale: pentachordal

t.c. G.

For mel. rel. see BES, 198(D); DV, 577, No. 24(H).

Barb'ry Allen

Tr. G. B.

It was in the spring - time of the year When flow-ers they were bloom-ing, A young man came from the north coun - try, Fell in love with Bar - b'ry Al - len.

Barb'ry Allen

It was in the springtime of the year
When flowers they were blooming,

A young man came from the north country,
Fell in love with Barb'ry Allen.

He sent his footman to her house,
Unto her house and dwelling,
Saying, "Arise, arise and come with me
If your name be Barb'ry Allen."

It's slowly, slowly she got up
And slowly she put on it
And slowly, slowly she arose
And slowly she went with him,

Until she came into his house
And to his house and dwelling,
And the very first words that e'er she spoke
Was, "I fear, young man, you're dying."

"A dying man I am not yet.
One kiss from you will cure me."
"One kiss from me you ne'er will get
If your poor heart was breaking.

"You remember last Saturday night
When in the tavern drinking,
You drank a health to all fair maids
And slighted Barb'ry Allen."

"Yes, I remember last Saturday night
When in the tavern drinking,
I drank a health to all fair maids
But remembered Barb'ry Allen.

"Look up, look up at my bed's head.
You'll see a gold watch hanging.
My gold watch and precious chain,
Give them to Barb'ry Allen.

"Look down, look down at my bed's foot.
You'll see a basin standing.

It overflows with my heart's blood,
I shed for Barb'ry Allen."

As she walked in her father's woods
She heard the dead bell ringing
And every toll the death bell gave
Was "hard-hearted Barb'ry Allen."

As she walked in her father's lawn
She saw the corpse a-coming.
"Lay down, lay down the corpse," she said,
"That I may look upon him."

The corpse was laid down at her feet.
There she stood a-laughing.
"Oh, fie, for shame," her friends all cried,
"Hard-hearted Barb'ry Allen!"

"Go make my bed, mama," she said,
"Oh, make it soft and mellow
For a young man died for me last night
And I'll die for him tomorrow."

"Oh, dig my grave, papa," she said,
"And dig it deep and narrow,
For a young man died for me last night
And I'll die for him tomorrow." [1]

One was buried in the middle of the church,
The other, in Mary's Abbey.
Out of one there grew a rose
And out of the other a briar.

And every night at twelve o'clock
They twined in a true lover's knot
The red rose and the briar

[1] On July 13 the last two lines of this stanza were given as,

"And plant it o'er with laurel leaves
That you may think upon me.

ANCIENT BALLADS

266

H[1]

The words of this song were furnished by Adam Johnson of Mooer's Forks, New York. Thomas Armstrong of Springfield, Vermont, knew the tune. Mr. Johnson learned this ballad when a child from a lady in Mooer's Forks who was born in Ireland. See H[2] and H[3].

H. H. F., Collector
March 20, 1935

Barbara Allen

It was early, early in the month of May,
When the trees were ripe and mellow,
That a young man lay a-dying on his bed
For the love of Barbara Allen.
That a young man lay a-dying on his bed,
For the love of Barbara Allen.

Then quickly, quickly she came to him
At the place where he was dwelling
And said as she drew the curtains aside,
"Poor boy, I am sorry you are dying."
        (Repeat last two lines for each verse

"Not dying yet, not dying yet,
One kiss from you will save me."
"One kiss from me you never shall receive,
While on your death-bed lying.

"Do you remember last Saturday night,
When in the ale-house drinking,
You drank your health to all the pretty maids,
And you slighted me, Barbara Allen?"

"Yes, I remember last Saturday night
While in the ale-house drinking,
I drank my health to all the pretty maids
And I slighted you, Barbara Allen.

"Look down, look down at the foot of my bed,
There you'll see a basin setting,
And in it is poured my heart's pure blood,
Which I shed for you, Barbara Allen."

As she was going from the room,
She turned and said unto him,
"I cannot keep you from your doom;
Farewell," said Barbara Allen.

He turned his face unto the wall,
As deadly pangs he fell in;
"Adieu! Adieu! Adieu to you all,
Adieu to Barbara Allen."

As she was walking o'er the fields
She heard the bell a-knellin'
And every stroke did seem to say,
"Unworthy Barbara Allen."

She turned her body around about
And spied the corpse a-comin'.
"Lay down, lay down the corpse," she said,
"That I may look upon him."

With scornful eye she looked down,
Her cheeks with laughter swellin'
Whilst all her friends cried out amain,
"Unworthy Barbara Allen."

When he was dead and laid in grave,
Her heart was struck with sorrow;
"O mother, mother, make my bed
For I shall die tomorrow.

"Hard-hearted creature, him to slight
Who loved me oh, so dearly,
Oh, had I been more kind to him
When he was alive and near me!"

She on her death-bed as she lay
Begged to be buried by him
And sore repented of the day
That she did e'er deny him.

"Farewell," she said, "ye virgins all,
And shun the fault I fell in;
Henceforth take warning by the fall
Of cruel Barbara Allen."

H²

*As sung by Mrs. Hattie Wilson of Springfield, Vermont,
sister of Thomas Armstrong. Learned from Adam Johnson
of Mooer's Forks, New York, whose version is H¹.*

H. H. F., *Collector*
March 31, 1935

Structure: A Bᵃ C D (2,2,2,2); Rhythm C; Contour: arc;
Scale: major

t.c. F.

For mel. rel. see Sharp 1, 181(L).

Barbara Allen

Tr. H. H. F.

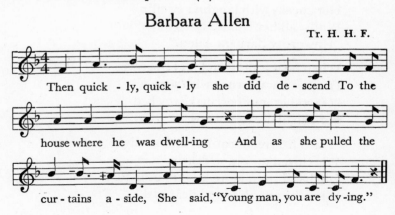

Then quick - ly, quick - ly she did de - scend To the
house where he was dwell-ing And as she pulled the
cur - tains a - side, She said, "Young man, you are dy -ing."

Barbara Allen

Then quickly, quickly she did descend
To the house where he was dwelling
And as she pulled the curtains aside,
She said, "Young man, you are dying."

"Not dying yet, not dying yet,
One kiss from you will save me."
"One kiss from me you never will receive,
While on your death bed lying.

"Do you remember last Saturday night
When in the ale-house drinking
You drank your health to all the pretty maids
And you slighted me, Barbara Allen?"

"Yes, I remember last Saturday night
While in the ale-house drinking,
I drank my health to all the pretty maids
And I slighted you, Barbara Allen."

        .   .   .   .

"O mother, mother, make my bed,
Go make it long and narrow,
For my true love died for me today
And I'll die for him tomorrow."

H^3

As sung by Thomas E. Armstrong of Mooer's Forks, New York, who at one time was a resident of Springfield, Vermont. Mr. Armstrong learned this ballad from Adam Johnson of Mooer's Forks, New York. See version H¹.

                    H. H. F., Collector
                    March 31, 1935

Structure: A B C D (2,2,2,2); Rhythm C but divergent;
Contour: arc; Scale: major

t.c. F.

Barb'ry Allen

Tr. M. O.

It was ear - ly, ear - ly in the month of May, When the trees were ripe and mel - low That a young man lay a - dy - ing on his bed, For the love of Bar - b'ry Al - len.

Barb'ry Allen

It was early, early in the month of May
When the trees were ripe and mellow
That a young man lay a-dying on his bed
For the love of Barb'ry Allen.
That a young man lay a-dying on his bed
For the love of Barb'ry Allen.

I

*Mrs. Frank Creaser of Ludlow remembered these words as
sung by her mother, Ellen Cunningham Sheahan of County
Waterford, Ireland, who lived as a girl in Keene, New*

Hampshire and later was employed at the Brattleboro Hotel owned by Jim Fiske. She married and settled in Cavendish, living there to the good old age of 104.

H. H. F., *Collector*
September 21, 1939

Barbry Ellen

It was in the springtime of the year
When the flowers were all in blossom
A young man from the north countree
Fell in love with Barbry Ellen;
A young man from the north countree
Fell in love with Barbry Ellen.

This young man was sick, oh, very, very sick,
And was almost a-dying.
He sent his postman all in post haste
And to Barbry Ellen's dwellings.
(Repeat last two lines of each verse)

"Get up, get up," the postman cried,
"My master he is dying.
Get up, get up," the postman cried,
"If you are Barbry Ellen."

Oh, slowly, slowly she got up
And slowly she was coming
And the very first look she gave at him
She said, "Young man, you're dying."

"A dying man I am not yet.
One kiss from you will cure me.
One kiss from you will cure me well
If you are Barbry Ellen."

"One kiss from me you never shall get
If I thought you were a-dying,

For don't you remember last Saturday night
When you were in the alehouse drinking,
You drank a health to each damsel 'round
And slighted Barbry Ellen."

He turned his face unto the wall,
Whilst death was o'er him dwelling.
"Take my gold watch and my gold chain;
Give them to Barbry Ellen."

She went right home to her mama's house
And she saw the dark clouds coming.
"Lay down the corpse, young men," she cried,
"Until I gaze upon him."

They laid down the corpse without allay.
In his face she fell a-laughing.
"Oh, fie, Oh, fie," the young men cried,
"If you are Barbry Ellen."

She went right home to her mama's house
And her heart was full of sorrow,
Saying, "A young man died for me today
And I'll die for him tomorrow."

J

*Contributed by mail by Mrs. Michael Mulcahy of Rutland,
Vermont, as learned in her girlhood in Ireland.*

*H. H. F., Collector
November 15, 1955*

Barbara Allen

Slowly, slowly she got up
And slowly she was dressing
And slowly she came into the room
Where this young man was lying,

And not a word came out of her mouth
But, "I hear, young man, you're dying."

"Now I'm sick and very bad
And on my death bed lying,
And one kiss from you will bring me through
If your name is Barbara Allen."

"Well, now, you're sick and very bad,
And on your death bed lying.
But one kiss from me you'll never get
Though my name is Barbara Allen."

"Look up, look up, at the head of my bed,
Where my gold watch is hanging.
Look down, look down, at the foot of my bed,
There's a silver basin standing
Where I threw up my whole heart's blood,
For the love of Barbara Allen."

"Remember the day at yon green hill
When all fair maids were gathered,
You drank a toast to everyone
And slighted Barbara Allen?

"Now turn your pale face to the wall
For death is creeping on you,
And bid adieu to the world's fair maids
And adieu to Barbara Allen."

She was scarcely three miles out of town
When she heard the death bells ringing
And every sound the death bell gave,
Was "Woe to Barbara Allen."

She said, "Mother, mother, make my bed;
Oh, make it long and narrow.
A young man died for me yesterday
And I'll die for him tormorrow."

K¹

As sung by Mrs. Lena Bourne Fish of East Jaffrey, New Hampshire. Her address was furnished by Mrs. Carl L. Schrader, Chairman of Fine Arts, General Federation of Women's Clubs.

M. Olney, Collector
May 9, 1940

Barbara Allen

It was in the merry month of May,
When the leaves were swelling,
That William on his death bed lay
For the love of Barbary Allen.

He sent his servant to a town
To the place where she was dwelling;
"My master's sick and sends for you;
Please do come, Barbary Allen."

She went but did not want to go,
Could hardly keep from crying,
But all she said when she got there
Was, "Young man, I think you're dying."

"I am sick, so very sick,
With my love my head is aching;
If you will but forgive your love
You'll keep my heart from breaking."

"Mind you not, young man," said she,
"When drinking in the tavern,
You drank a health to ladies all,
But slighted Barbary Allen.

"I know you're sick and very sick,
And death is with you dealing,

But I will never you forgive,
Though death shades are 'round you stealing."

He turned his face unto the wall,
She turned so coldly from him;
He bade adieu to the wide world all
And adieu to Barbary Allen.

As she was walking to her home,
She heard the death bells knelling,
And every peal the death bell gave
Meant woe to Barbary Allen.

"O sexton, go and dig my grave,
Dig it both long and narrow;
My lover died for me of love,
I'll die for him of sorrow."

K^2

This text was also given by Mrs. Lena Bourne Fish of East Jaffrey, New Hampshire, as learned from her father, Stratton Bourne. It is included in full as it differs quite markedly in phrasing from K^1 and demonstrates how freely some singers change their songs.

M. Olney, Collector
May 9, 1940

Barbara Allen

'Twas in the merry month of May
When the green buds were swelling,
That William on his death bed lay
For the love of Barb'ry Allen.

He sent his servant up in haste
To the place where she was dwelling,
Saying, "William's sick and calls for you;
Please come, dear Barb'ry Allen."

She walked out with a haughty air
Although she felt like crying,
But all she said when she got there,
Was, "Young man, I fear you're dying."

"Oh, I am sick, so very sick,
With fever I am shaking;
If you will only smile on me
'Twill keep my heart from breaking."

"I know you're sick, so very sick,
And death is with you dealing,
But I will never smile on you,
Nor will I be your healing.

"For mind you not, young man," said she,
"When the gay May bells were knelling,
You drank a toast to the ladies all around,
But slighted Barb'ry Allen."

"Though I drank a toast to the ladies all,
When the gay May bells were knelling,
But my truest, best and constant love,
I gave to Barb'ry Allen."

He bade this cruel world adieu
When she turned coldly from him;
And walked away with an air of pride,
Hard-hearted Barbara Allen.

Before she reached her dwelling place,
She heard the death bell knelling
And every peal the death bell gave,
Meant woe to Barb'ry Allen.

L

As sung by Franklin Smith to his son, Herbert Wilson Smith, of Washington, D.C., who often spent much time

with his father in New England. Copied literatim et punc-
tatim from handwritten sheets given by the father to his
son in 1918.

H. H. F., *Collector*
August 7, 1957

Barby Ellen

Twas in the happy month of May
When green buds all are swelling
This well favored lad did pine away
For love of Barby Ellen

He sent his bound man with his word
Unto fair Barby Ellen
"O you must to my master hie
Lest he die while this I'm telling"

So slowly slowly came she up
So slowly came she nigh him
To him she said when she got there
"Young man I think you're dying"

He turned his face to look her straight
His heart with love was swelling
"O fair young maid pray pity me
O Lovely Barby Ellen."

"Do you think back to Christmas Day
Greens hung in every dwelling
You sang and bussed the other (girls) maids
But never Barby Ellen."

Again his pale face to the wall
"Again my love I'm telling
Not for the other pretty maids
But only Barby Ellen."

She walked then home across the lea
She heard the church bells knelling
Cold death had taken him away
For love of Barby Ellen.

"O Mother dear make my death bed
For I shall die tomorrow
That fair young man he died of love
And I shall die of sorrow

And to young maidens near and far
Pray take this solemn warning
Let not your hearts go cold with pride
As did poor Barby Ellen."

M

As sung by Albert Cox of Sherman Mills, Maine.

M. Olney, Collector
May 10, 1942

Barb'ry Allen

'Twas on the fourteenth day of May,
When all things were a-blooming,
A young man on his death bed lay
In love with Barb'ry Allen.
He sent a boy three miles from town
Unto his lady's dwelling,
Saying, "Uncle dear has sent me here
In the name of Barb'ry Allen."

So slowly she put on her clothes
And so slowly she came unto him,
And all that she said to him was,
"Young man, I fear you're dying!
And are you ill and are you may?
For there's no need of talking,

For you will be none the better of me,"
Says cruel Barb'ry Allen.

"Oh, don't you remember the other night
We were at the bar a-drinking?
You passed your glasses 'round and around
And you slighted Barb'ry Allen.
And don't you remember the other night
We were at the hall a-dancing?
You held another pretty girl on your knee
And you slighted Barb'ry Allen?"

He turned his face towards the wall
And he turned his back unto her,
Saying, "I bid adieu to all this earth
But it's woe to Barb'ry Allen."
She'd scarcelie gone three miles from town
When she heard the death bell tolling
And as it tolled she heard it roll,
"O cruel Barb'ry Allen!"

Oh, she looked east and she looked west
And she saw the corpse a-coming.
She says, "Lie down, you corpse,
While I now gaze upon him.
Oh, cruel be my lot
And cruel be my nature.
I might have saved that young man's life
By trying my endeavor!"

"O mother, dear, go make me a bed,
Go make it long and narrow;
Since my love died for me today,
I will die for him tomorrow.
O mother, dear, go dig me a grave,
Go dig it long and narrow;
Since my love died for me today,
I will die for him tomorrow."

N

Sung by Mrs. Hattie E. Smith of Springfield, Maine, who said: "My father taught me this song when I was a little girl, five or six years old."

M. Olney, Collector
September 2, 1942

Structure: stanza 1, A^1 A^2 A^2 B (2, 2, 2, 2)—stanza 2, E^1 E^2 F G^1—stanza 3, M N O G^2—stanza 4, R S T U; Rhythm C; Contour: each stanza an arc; Scale: stanza 1, hexatonic; t.c. E—stanza 2, major; t.c. first E, then C—stanza 3, anhemitonic pentatonic; t.c. D—stanza 4, anhemitonic pentatonic; t.c. C.

For mel. rel. see possibly FCB4, 62 (G) for stanza 1; for others, see "Old Lang Syne."

Barbara Allen

Tr. H. E. F. B.

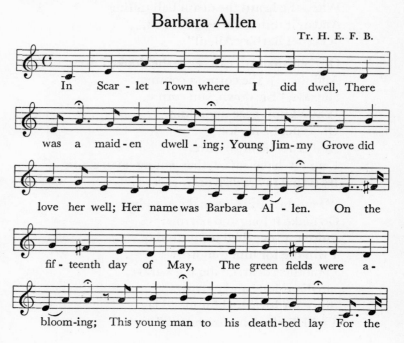

In Scar-let Town where I did dwell, There was a maid-en dwell-ing; Young Jim-my Grove did love her well; Her name was Barbara Al-len. On the fif-teenth day of May, The green fields were a-bloom-ing; This young man to his death-bed lay For the

love of Bar-bara Al - len. So slow (ly) she put
on her gown, So slow - ly she went to him; And
all she said when she got there Was, "Young man, you
are a - dy - ing, For death is print - ed
on your face, And sor - row on your bear - ing; You
nev - er will be none the bet - ter for
me, Nor the love of Bar - bara Al - len."

The remaining stanzas are pretty consistent to the tune of the last
stanza, which seems to be a variant of the tune of "Auld Lang Syne"

Barbara Allen

In Scarlet Town where I did dwell,
There was a maiden dwelling;
Young Jimmy Grove did love her well;
Her name was Barbara Allen.

On the fifteenth day of May,
The green fields were a-blooming;

This young man to his death-bed lay
For the love of Barbara Allen.

So slowly she put on her gown,
So slowly she went to him;
And all she said when she got there
Was, "Young man, you are a-dying.

"For death is printed on your face
And sorrow on your bearing;
You never will be none the better for me,
Nor the love of Barbara Allen."

She had not got far out of town
Before the bells were tolling,
And with the tolling of the bells
Laughed cruel Barbara Allen.

She turned about to get her breath
And spied the funeral coming;
She laughed to see him pale in death.
O cruel Barbara Allen!

When he was buried in his grave,
Her heart did burst with sorrow.
"O mother, mother, make my bed,
For I shall die tomorrow!

"Now, maidens all, a warning take
And shun the way I fell in,
Or else your heart like mine will break;
Farewell!" said Barbara Allen.

O

*This fragment was sung by Mrs. Annie Sawyer in Fairfax,
Vermont.*

*H. H. F., Collector
September 11, 1955*

Barbara Allen

[*She left the room. He sends for her. She accuses him of going out with someone else.*]

Slowly, slowly, she got up
And slowly she put on her clothes.
[*And she went into the room where her young man was lying. He sent for her.*]

Slowly, slowly, she came in
To the room where he was lying
And not a word came out of her mouth
But, "I hear, young man, you are dying."

[*She had gone.*]

She heard the bells a-tolling
And every sound the death knell gave
"Return, Barbara Allen."

"Mother, mother, make my bed;
Make it long and narrow
For a young man died for me last night
And I'll die for him tomorrow."

And out of her grew a red rose
And out of him, a briar.

P

As sung in Springfield, Vermont, by Mrs. Peggy Coffin Halvosa of Barre, Vermont, formerly of Brunswick, Maine, as sung to her by her father, Robert P. Tristram Coffin, of Brunswick, Maine.

H. H. F., Collector
July 27, 1957

Structure: A B C D (2,2,2,2); Rhythm E; Contour: arc;
Scale: major

t.c. F.

For mel. rel. see DV, 577, No. 24(G).

Barbara Allen

Tr. H. E. F. B.

moth - er, make my bed. Oh, make it soft and nar - row. My love he died for me to - day; I'll die for him to - mor - row."

Barbara Allen

In Scarlet Town, where I was born,
There was a fair maid dwelling
Made all the youths cry, "Well away,"
And her name was Barb'ra Allen.

Oh, Danny Groves on his death bed lay
And death was with him dwelling.
"Adieu, adieu, my good friends all,
And be kind to Barb'ry Allen."

"O mother, mother, make my bed.
Oh, make it soft and narrow.
My love he died for me today;
I'll die for him tomorrow."

Q

A fragment as learned from her forebears by Mrs. John Fairbanks of North Springfield, Vermont. Her mother was Margaret Kelley, born in Ireland.

H. H. F., Collector
October 5, 1939

Structure: A B C D (2,2,2,2); Rhythm B; Contour: arc;
Scale: hexachordal

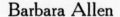

t.c. B-flat. Note the small range (major sixth).

For mel. rel. see Sharp 1, 191(I); DV, 579, No. 24(FF);
MF, 287.

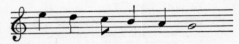

Barbara Allen

Tr. M. O.

Barbara Allen

In Scarlet Town where I was born
There was a fair maid dwelling,
Made ev'ry lad cry well-a-day;
Her name was Barb'ra Allen.

He sent his servant to the house
Where Barbara Allen was dwelling,
Saying, "Arise, arise, my pretty fair maid,
Your true love, he is dying."

"Arise, arise," her father did cry,
"Arise and go and see him."

"Oh, never mind, dear father," she cried,
"It is often you told me 'leave him.' "

"Arise, arise," her mother did cry,
"Arise and go and see him."
"Oh, never mind, dear mother," she cried,
"You often bade me 'leave him.' "

R

*Orlon Merrill of Charlestown, New Hampshire, formerly
a trapper, guide, and woodsman, who turned village carpenter, sang this fragment as learned from his mother, who had
previously lived in Canada. The second stanza was printed
in the Springfield, Mass.,* Republican, *August 9, 1931.*

H. H. F., *Collector*
1931

Structure: A B C D (2,2,2,2); Rhythm E; Contour: arc, but
pendulumlike; Scale: major

t.c. F.

For mel. rel. see Sharp 1, 183; RO 1, 128.

Barb'ry Allen

Tr. M. O.

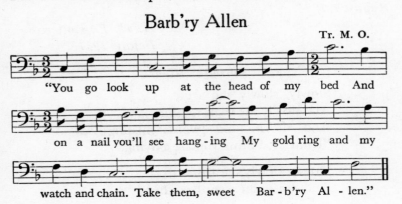

Barb'ry Allen

.   .   .   .

"When a kiss from you would cure me."
"A kiss from me, that never shall be,
Not if your poor heart is breaking."

"You go look up at the head of my bed
And on a nail you'll see hanging
My gold ring and my watch and chain.
Take them, sweet Barb'ry Allen."

"O mother, go and make my bed;
Make it long and narrow,
For a young man died for me last night
And I'll die for him tomorrow."

When she came home, it was late at night;
She heard the church bell tolling
And every toll, it seemed to say,
"Hard-hearted Barb'ry Allen!'

S

These lines of "Barbara Allen" were sent by Josiah Kennison of Townshend, Vermont. See Springfield, Mass., Republican, *August 9, 1931.*

H. H. F., Collector
Before 1931

Barbara Allen

Slowly, slowly she arose
And slowly she went to him
And all she said [words missing] was
"Kind sir, I think you are a-dying."

Slowly, slowly she arose
And slowly she went from him.

T

As sung by Mrs. Anna Rainsford French Bush of Concord,
Massachusetts. Learned from a friend who had learned it
from a nurse in the family. It was traditional in the nurse's
family. Mrs. Bush mentioned the ballad in a letter to
H. H. F. dated November 26, 1954.

M. Olney, Collector
November 30, 1954

Structure: A B A C (2,2,2,2); Rhythm C; Contour: inverted
arc; Scale: Dorian

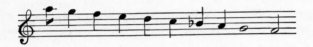

t.c. G.

For mel. rel. see EO, 52; FCB4, 62(G); BES, 195; Sharp 1,
191(G and H); DV, 580, No. 24(II and JJ); RO 1, 131, 134;
BI, 106.

Barberry Allen

Tr. M. O.

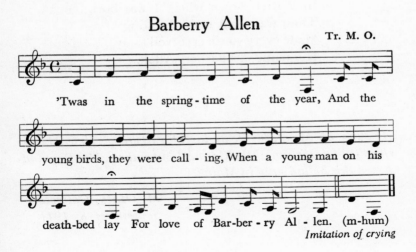

'Twas   in   the spring-time   of   the year, And the

young birds, they were call - ing, When a young man on his

death-bed lay For love of Bar-ber - ry Al - len. (m-hum)
Imitation of crying

Barberry Allen

'Twas in the springtime of the year
And the young birds they were calling
When a young man on his death-bed lay
For the love of Bar-ber-ry Allen. (m-hum)

U

*The following is copied from a manuscript book of music
and texts purchased for the files of the Flanders Ballad
Collection by Mrs. W. H. Beardsley of Springfield, Vermont,
August 6, 1951. It is incomplete; begins at page 23. On
page 50 is "Charles Webbs Book 1798"; on page 104 "Wind-
ham Connecticut March 1800. C L Webb"; further on is
"Charles H. Webb Litchfield February 21, 1826."*

Barbery Allen

In Scarlet Town where I was born
Their was a fair maid dwelling
Made every youth crye well away
Her name was Barbery Allen.

V

*As sung by Maynard Reynolds of Pittsburg, New Hamp-
shire (upper section of the Connecticut Lakes). Mr. Reynolds
heard this ballad sung in Maine.*

M. Olney, Collector
September 8, 1941

Structure: A B C D (2,2,2,2); **Rhythm** E; **Contour:** arc; **Scale:** anhemitonic pentatonic

t.c. C.

For mel. rel. see DV, 577, No. 24(H); FCB 4, 59(A) (4), 64(S), (S, 1); SSC, 132; Sharp 1, 185; MF, 285; RO 1, 136.

Barb'ra Allen

"O father, O father, go dig my grave,
Go dig it long and narrow;
Young William died for pure, pure love,
And Barb'ra died for sorrow."

Oh, she was buried in the old churchyard
And he was buried by her;
On William's grave grew a big red rose;
On Barbar's grew a green briar.

Barb'ra Allen

Tr. M. O.

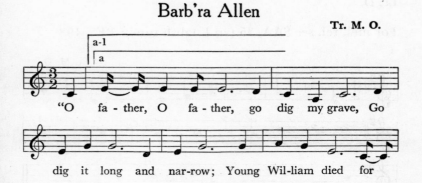

They grew upon the old church wall
Till they couldn't grow any higher;
They 'twined themselves in a true-lover's knot,
The rose around the briar.

W

Tune only by Evelyn Braid of Providence, Rhode Island.

M. Olney, Collector

Structure: A B C D (2,2,2,2); Rhythm E; Contour: arc;
Scale: major

t.c. **D.**

For mel. rel. see SAA, 35 (an English tune); BES, 198.

Tr. M. O.

Young Johnstone

(Child 88)

This song, to this writer's knowledge, has not been un-covered from oral tradition in the United States, although W. Roy MacKenzie, *Ballads and Sea-Songs from Nova Scotia* (Cambridge, Mass., 1928), 41 f., found Child C and D variants in Canada. *The Charms of Melody* text clearly has had no oral tradition. Besides the fact that it is copied from print, it is a close replica, even to its title, of the D. Herd, *Ancient and Modern Scottish Songs* (Edinburgh, 1776), I, 165, "Cruel Knight" (Child A). Child stanzas 8 and 9 are omitted in *The Charms of Melody* text, and stanzas 3 and 11 contain slight modifications. Otherwise, the spelling and phrasing of the copied text and Child A are identi-cal, allowing for a remarkably slight degree of modernization.

The original story of the song cannot be read from *The Charms of Melody* variant. The knight, Young Johnstone, has killed his sweetheart's brother because this gentleman has made slurring remarks about Johnstone's sister. After the crime, he flees to the home of this sister where he is told he will surely have to hang for the killing. He then decides to ride to the home of his sweetheart, the dead man's sister, where he is hidden in spite of his deed. When the King's guards come after Johnstone and describe him, the girl loyally tells them he has hurried on a while before. As they rush off in pursuit, she goes to tell Johnstone what she has done, startles him from his sleep, and is stabbed. He immediately regrets his rashness and promises her the best medical aid. She, however, dies.

Coffin, 93-94, includes a brief discussion of this ballad, but the song is so rare there is little to refer a reader to beyond Child.

Copied literatim et punctatim by H. H. F. from a compilation of 400 pages of numbered issues of The Charms of Melody: *or* Siren Medley, *printed by J. & J. Carrick, Bachelor's Walk, Dublin. The watermark on the title page reads* GREAT NEWTON, *with the date 1818. Copies are available at the Boston Athenaeum; the John Hay Library at Brown University (60 pages, dated 1824, beginning with Volume 1, page 1); and at the Library of Congress.*

H. H. F., Collector
August 1, 1958

The Cruel Knight.

THE knight ftands in the ftable door
   As he was bownd to ride;
Whan out thair comes his fair lady,
   And him defires to bide.

"How can I bide, how dare I bide,
   "How can I bide wi thee?
"Have I not kill'd thy ae brother?
   "Thou hadft nae mair but he."

"If thou haft kill'd my ae brother,
   "Alas and wae is me!
"But if I fave thee from the paine,
   "My luve's the mair to thee."

She has taen him to her fecret bower,
   Steik'd wi a filler-pin:

And fhe's up to the higheft tower,
    To watch that nane come in.

She had nae weil gane up the ftair,
    And entered in the tower,
When four and twenty armed knights
    Came riding to the door.

"Now God you fave, my fair lady,
    "Declare to me, I pray,
"Did you not fee a wounded knight
    "Come riding by this way?

"Yes, bloody bloody was his fword,
    "And bloody were his hands;
"But, if the fteed he rides be good,
    "He's paft fair Scotland's ftrands."

Then fhe's gane to her darkfome bower,
    Her hufband dear to meet;
He deem'd he heard his angry faes,
    And wounded her fou deep.

"What harm my lord provokes thine ire,
    "To wreak itfelf on me?
"Have I not fav'd thy life frae faes,
    "And fav'd for fic a fee!"

"Now live, now live, my fair lady,
    "O live but half an hour;
"There's neer a leech in all Scotland
    "But fhall be at thy bower."

"How can I live, how fhall I live,
    "How can I live for thee?
"While running faft o'er a the floor,
    "My heart's blood thou may'ft fee!"

Lamkin

(Child 93)

Although Child printed twenty-six versions of "Lamkin"
and although it is still known in British-American tradition,
the story of the revengeful mason who murders a woman
and child because he has not been paid is much the same
wherever it is found. The fact that the crime is so weakly
motivated has made scholars suspect much of the plot to be
lost. Phillips Barry (see *JAF*, LII, 70-74) offers an appealing
explanation in connection with the "False Linfinn" text
(Flanders B) collected in Maine. "The Linfinn" was Irish for
"the white man who lives by the stream," the outcast who
was a leper forced to live alone. A cure for leprosy could be
had through the blood of an innocent human collected in
a silver container, and this fact offers a real motive for the
crime. Barry felt that the identification of Linfinn with
masonry came later, possibly because Irish masons had a
recipe for making cement with blood. However, other
scholars have identified the name Lamkin as a Flemish
form of Lambert and noted that Flemish masons were well-
known in Britain in the Middle Ages. In America, one
Virginia informant noted by Arthur K. Davis in his *Traditional Ballads of Virginia* (Cambridge, Mass., 1929), 357,
claimed there had been a love affair between the lady and
the mason prior to the opening of the story. Whatever the
answer, the crime seems rather extreme as a retaliation for
failure to pay a debt.

Flanders A has the false window built by the irate mason
(Child E), and A, B, and C contain the offer of the

daughter's hand as a bribe (Child F, T, X). In D¹, D², E, and F only gold is proffered. A, B, D¹, D², and F include the basin of blood, and all the Flanders texts find the false nurse or maid executed with Lamkin at the end. These points generally ally the New England tradition printed here with the Child B, C, F group and the material discussed in Barry, *British Ballads from Maine,* 203-6, although the Flanders H fragment, where the nurse actually lets the murderer in, recalls the Child A story. For other discussions and bibliography, start with Coffin, 94-96 (American); Dean-Smith, 83 (English); and Greig and Keith, 71-72 (Scottish).

The Flanders G text, "Tumkin" (Tom King), with its relationship to Dick Turpin legends, is interesting, if hard to explain.

All of the tunes for Child 93 are members of the same family. The Moses and Delorme tunes are slightly removed from the rest, the Delorme tune being related primarily at the first line. For melodic relationship to the entire group, see FCB4, 74-76 (all tunes for Child 93); Sharp 1, 202, 204, 205; EO, 59; DV, 583, No. 26 (B); BES, 201 (especially related to the Delorme tune); and GCM, 313 (distant).

A

Printed in JAF, LII, 70-74, with extensive notes on how it was collected. Text from Mrs. Margaret (McPhail) Morris, of Kingman, Maine. Mrs. Morris was born in Charlottetown, P.E.I., in 1853, and probably learned the song of her mother, Ruth (Hescot) McPhail, who was born in England about 1812 and died in St. John, N.B., about 1905, aged 93. The air was recorded on the dictaphone by Phillips Barry from the singing of Adam Morris.

Fannie Hardy Eckstorm, Collector
August 20, 1934

Lamkin

Lamkin was as fine a mason as e'er laid a stone;
Built a castle for Lord Warrington and payment he got
    none.

O, he built it all round and he lined it within,
And he left a false window for himself to creep in.

The lord of his castle was going away;
"Beware of Bold Lamkin," to his lady did say.

"I care not for Lamkin or none of his kin,
For my doors are all bolted and my windows pinned in."

In the middle of the night Bold Lamkin crept in;
"Good morning, Bold Lamkin," said the false nurse to him.

"Where is the Lord of the castle, or is he within?"
"He's gone over to London to dine with the King."

"O, where are his noblemen, or are they within?"
"They've gone over to London to wait upon him."

"Where is his lady, or is she within?"
"She's up in her chamber with her windows penned in."

"How can we get her down?" the Lamkin did cry;
"Kill her baby in the cradle," the false nurse replied.[1]

" 'Tis a pity, 'tis a pity," the Lamkin did cry;
"No pity, no pity," the false nurse replied.

The Lamkin did rock and the false nurse did sing,
In four corners of the cradle the red blood did spring.

"I can't please your baby with breast-milk or pap,
O, pray, dearest lady, come take it in your lap."

---

[1] Mrs. Morris explained that the false nurse was a cousin to Bold
Lamkin and that they "stuck a bobkin in the soft spot in the baby's head."

"How can I come down this cold, bitter night,
Without one speck of fire or a candle light?"

"The moon's on the stairway as bright as the sun;
Why can't a fair lady be lighted by one?"

"Nurse, dearest nurse, how cruel you be;
If your head only ached, how sorry I'd be."

"Please spare my life till one o'clock,
You shall have my daughter Betsy, she's the flower of my
      flock."

"Call down your daughter Betsy and set her at work,
To scour out the basin that holds your heart's blood."

There's blood on the stairway, there's blood in the hall,
There's blood in the nursery, the best blood of all.

As Betsy was sitting in her chamber most high
She saw her father come riding thereby.

"O father, dear father, don't you blame me,
For the false nurse and Lamkin has slain your ladye."

The Lamkin was hung on the gallows so high,
And the false nurse was burnt on the mountain near by.

It was Scotland's lamentation and Ireland's loud cry,
"Hushaby, lullaby, hushaby, lullaby."

B

*Printed in JAF, LII, 70-74, with extensive notes on how it
was collected. From the singing of Mrs. Susan M. Harding,
Hampden, Maine. Air recorded on the dictaphone by
Phillips Barry. Mrs. Harding said that the song was from her
mother's family, the Knowltons, who came early from
England to Massachusetts.*
                         Fannie Hardy Eckstorm, Collector
                         June 16, 1934

False Linfinn

Said the lord to his lady as he went away from home,
"Beware of the Linfinn, for he'll do you much harm."

"I care not for Linfinn nor none of his kin,
I keep my doors bolted and my windows pinned in."

"How shall I get her down?"

.   .   .   .

They pricked it and they pricked it and they pricked it
    full sore
Till the blood ran from the cradle in streams on the floor.

"I've rocked it and fed it on breast milk and pap,
Why can't you come down and rock it on your lap?"

"How can I come down so late in the night
Without any fire or bright candlelight?"

"There are fifteen bright candles burning and one as bright
    as the sun;
You can come down here by the light of one of them!"

She started to come down, not thinking any harm,
And the Linfinn stood ready to catch her in his arms.

"O spare me, Mr. Linfinn, till one o'clock at night,
And you shall have as much money as you can carry in your
    cart."

"If I had as much money as I could haul in my cart,
I'd rather see a sword run through your red heart."

"O spare, O spare me, O spare me," she cries,
"And you shall have my daughter Betsy, she's the pride of
    all flowers."

"Bring down your daughter Betsy, she may do some good
For to hold the silver basin for to catch your heart's blood."

"O Betsy, dearest Betsy, stay right where you be,
Until your noble father comes a-riding home from sea."

As Betsy was a-sittin' in her chamber most high,
She saw her noble father come a-riding close by.

Says, "Father, dearest father, pray do not blame me,
For the Linfinn and the wet nurse has murdered Ma-mee."

The wet nurse was hung on the gallows so high,
And the Linfinn was burned to a stake standing by.[1]

"Farewell to old England, old Ireland," says he,
And the landlord went a-mourning for his fair ladye.

C

*As sung by Jonathan Moses of Orford, New Hampshire.
Learned from his father. Printed in* Ballads Migrant in New
England, *104.*

M. Olney, Collector
July 3, 1942

Structure: A B^a C D C D (2,2,2,2,2,2); Rhythm divergent;
Contour: inverted arc; Scale: anhemitonic pentatonic

t.c. C.

Squire Relantman

Squire Relantman was a fine mason
    As ever you see;
He built a fine castle;
    Lord Nelson got none.
    (*Last two lines of each stanza repeated*)

---

[1] The hanging of the nurse and the burning of Linfinn reverse the usual
pattern, probably due to a lapse of memory.

Squire Relantman

Tr. M. O.

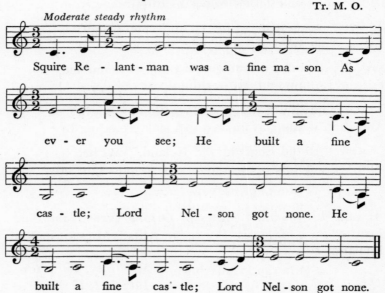

Squire Re - lant-man was a fine ma - son As ev - er you see; He built a fine cas - tle; Lord Nel - son got none. He built a fine cas'- tle; Lord Nel - son got none.

Lord Nelson was a-going
    For to sail far away;
He told his fair lady
    For to keep her own room.

Lord Nelson he started
    And he sailed far away;
Kitchen windows being left open,
    Squire Relantman crept in.

"Oh, where is Lord Nelson
    Or is he within?"
"He has sailed far away,"
    Said this fair maid unto him.

"Oh, where is his lady
    Or is she within?"

"She is locked in her chamber,"
  Said this fair maid unto him.

"Oh, how can I get to her
  Or how can I get in?"
"Stick a pin in her baby,"
  Says this fair maid unto him.

Squire Relantman rocked the cradle
  While this fair maid she did sing,
And out of his cradle
  His heart's blood did spin.

"I cannot please your baby,
  I cannot please him on the key;
I cannot please your baby;
  You must come down and see."

"How can I come down
  So late in ther night
While there's no candles a-burning
  Nor no fire light?"

"Although it is late,
  So late in ther night,
There is two candles a-burning
  And a good fire light."

This lady she started
  Her baby for to see;
Squire Relantman he met her
  And he brought her upon her knee.

"Oh, spare but my life
  Two hours or three.
You shall have my daughter Betsey,
  Fair a queen as you've seen.

"Daughter Betsey, daughter Betsey,
   Go on the towers so high
And see if your own dear father
   Ain't a-riding thereby."

Daughter Betsey, daughter Betsey
   Went on the towers so high;
There she saw her own dear father
   A-riding thereby.

"O father, onward father,
   Oh, ride without speed;
Squire Relantman's killed your own son,
   Your fair lady and me."

Squire Relantman was hung
   On the gallis so high;
This fair maid she was burned
   To a stake there nearby.

D^1

As sung by Mrs. Will Barry of Belvidere, Vermont. Both Mr. and Mrs. Barry were unable to recall where they learned this ballad but said they both learned it at the same time when they were young. See Text D².

M. Olney, Collector
August 21, 1941

Structure: A¹ A² B C (2,2,2,2); Rhythm C but divergent;
Contour: inverted arc; Scale: hexatonic

t.c. F.

False Lamkins

Tr. H. E. F. B.

False Lam - kins, as good a ma - son As
ev - er laid stone, He built Lord Farm - er's
cas - tle And the lord paid him none.

False Lamkins

False Lamkins, as good a mason
As ever laid stone,
He built Lord Farmer's castle
And the lord paid him none.

The lord says to his lady,
"I am going away;
So beware of False Lamkins;
Let no one betray."

"I am not afraid of False Lamkins
Nor any of his kin,
For my doors shall all be bolted
And my windows barred in."

The doors they were all bolted
And the windows barred in
Except the kitchen window
Where False Lamkins crawled in.

"Where the lord's lady,
Or is she within?"

"Yes, she's in her chamber sleeping
Where there's no one goes in."

"How shall I git up
Or how shall I git in?"
"I will break the babe to its heart
With a bright silver pin."

"Oh, hush my dear baby,
Oh, hush, I do say."
"No, I can't, my loving lady,
Till you come down and see."

She hadn't entered the first stair,
Nor the second, nor the third,
Before she met False Lamkins
With a glittering broadsword.

"False Lamkins, False Lamkins,
Oh, spare me, I pray,
And I'll give you as much gold
As you can carry away." [1]

"Will you give me as much gold
As I could pile on yonders deck,
It would not keep this broadsword
From your lily-white neck."

"O False Lamkins, False Lamkins,
Oh, spare me one hour
Till I call my daughter Betsey,
The queen of the bower."

"Oh, go call down your daughter Betsey,
She may do you some good;

[1] When Mrs. Barry was recorded a year later, September 24, 1942, she sang this stanza and the one following which she had recalled since August 1941.

She may hold the silver basin
For to catch your heart's blood."

Daughter Betsey, daughter Betsey
Run up a garret so high;
There she saw her own dear father
A-riding near by.

"O father, father,
Don't lay it to me;
False Lamkins and false nurse
Has killed your ladee.

"There is blood in the entry,
And there's blood in the hall;
There lies your loving lady
Down dead by the wall."

False Lamkins he was hung
On a gallus so high;
The false nurse she was burnt
In a furnace near by.

D^2

As sung by Will Barry of Belvidere, Vermont. During the singing he sometimes added an "s" to Lamkin. In another rendition Mr. Barry made slight verbal changes in stanza 6. See also Text D^1.

M. Olney, Collector
August 21, 1941

Structure: A^1 A^2 B C (2,2,2,2); Rhythm divergent; Contour: inverted arc; Scale: Lydian

t.c. F.

False Lamkin

Tr. H. E. F. B.

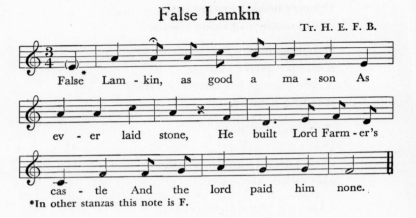

False   Lam - kin,   as   good   a   ma - son   As
ev - er   laid   stone,   He   built   Lord Farm - er's
cas - tle   And   the   lord   paid   him   none.

*In other stanzas this note is F.

False Lamkin

False Lamkin, as good a mason
As ever laid stone,
He built Lord Farmer's castle
And the lord paid him none.

"Oh," the lord said to his lady,
"I am going away.
Now, beware of False Lamkin.
Let no one betray."

"I'm not afraid of False Lamkins
Nor any of his kin
For my doors shall all be bolted
And the windows barred in."

The doors were all bolted
And the windows barred in
Except the kitchen window
Where False Lamkin crawled in.

"Oh, where's the lord's lady
Or is she within?"

"Yes, she's in her chamber sleeping
Where there's no one goes in."

"How shall I git up
And how shall I git in?"
"I will break the babe to its heart
With a bright silver pin."

"Oh, hush my dear baby.
Oh, hush, I do say."
"No, I can't, my loving lady,
Till you come down and see."

Before she entered the first stair
Nor the second, nor the third,
There she met False Lamkins
With a glittering broadsword.

"Oh, spare me, False Lamkins,
Oh, spare me one hour
Till I call my daughter Betsey,
The queen of the bower."

"Go call down your daughter Betsey.
She may do you some good.
She may hold the silver basin
For to catch your heart's blood."

Daughter Betsey ran upstairs
In the garret so high
There she saw her own dear father
A-riding near by.

"Dear father, dear father,
Don't lay it to me.
The false nurse, the False Lamkins
Has killed your ladee.

"There's blood in the entry;
There is blood in the hall;

There lies your loving lady
Down dead by the wall."

False Lamkins he was hung
On the gallows so high.
The false nurse she was burnt
In the furnace near by.

E

Sung by Jack Hoadley of Johnson, Vermont.

H. H. F., Collector
July 22, 1946

Structure: A¹ A² B C (2,2,2,2); Rhythm C but divergent;
Contour: inverted arc; Scale: major

t.c. F.

False Lamkin

Tr. H. E. F. B.

False Lam - kin's good a ma - son As
ev - er laid stone. He built Lord Farm-er's
cas - tle, And the lord paid him none.

False Lamkin

False Lamkin's good a mason
As ever laid stone.
He built Lord Farmer's castle,
And the lord paid him none.

Says the lord to his lady,
"I am going away
So beware of False Lamkin;
Let no one betray."

"I am not 'fraid of False Lamkin
Nor any of his kin
For my doors will all be bolted
And my windows barred in."

Her doors were all bolted
And her windows barred in,
Except the kitchen window
Where False Lamkin crawled in.

He had not got the first stair
Nor the second nor the third
Before she met False Lamkin
With a glittering broadsword;
Before she met False Lamkins
With a glittering broadsword.

"Oh, spare me, False Lamkins,
Oh, spare me one hour,
And I'll give you as much gold
As you carry away."

"If you'll give me as much gold
It would stand on yonder deck,
It will not keep the broadsword
From your lily-white neck." [1]

[1] Mrs. Ethel Hill of Johnson, Vermont, wrote that on June 28, 1954, Mr. Hoadley gave words for stanzas 6 and 7 as follows:

> "Oh, spare me, False Lamkins,
> Oh, spare me, I pray,
> And I will give to you as much gold
> As you will carry away."
>
> "Oh, if you gave me as much gold
> As would stand on yonders deck,
> It would not keep the broadsword
> From your lily-white neck."

Daughter Betsy ran upstairs
In the garret so high;
There she saw her own dear father
A-riding near by.
There she saw her own dear father
A-riding near by.

"O father, dear father,
Don't lay it to me.
The false nurse and False Lamkin
Has killed your lady.

"There is blood in the entry,
There is blood in the hall,
There lies your loving lady
Down dead by the wall."

False Lamkin he was hung
On the gallows so high;
The false nurse she was burned
In a furnace near by.

F

As sung by Mrs. Lily M. Delorme of Cadyville, New York.
Mrs. Delorme was born in Schuyler Falls, New York, in
1869. Her father was born in Starksboro, Vermont; her
mother, in Schuyler Falls. This ballad was learned in her
home as a child.

M. Olney, Collector
December 8, 1941

Structure: A B C D (2,2,2,2); Rhythm C but divergent;
Contour: each half an arc: Scale: hexatonic

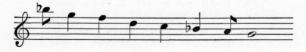

t.c. C.

Tr. H. E. F. B.

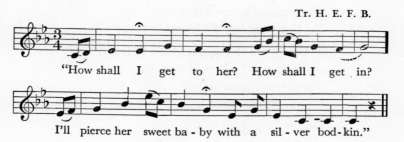

"How shall I get to her? How shall I get in?
I'll pierce her sweet ba-by with a sil-ver bod-kin."

False Lamkin

["*The first of this ballad I can recollect is where False Lam-kin says to the false maid,*"]

> "How shall I get to her,
>   How shall I get in?"
> "I'll pierce her sweet baby
>   With a silver bodkin."

["*The next I recollect is where he has got in and the lady says,*"]

> "O Lamkin, dear Lamkin,
>   Spare me till one o'clock,
> And I'll give you all the money
>   You can carry on your back."

> "Oh, no," said False Lamkin,
>   "I'll not spare you till one o'clock,
> Not for all of the money
>   I could carry on my back."

> "O Lamkin, dear Lamkin,
>   Spare me but one hour,
> Till I call my daughter Betsy
>   To see this brown flower."

> "You may call your daughter Betsy
>   And send her again

To fetch a silver basin
  For your heart's blood to run in."

"Daughter Betsy, daughter Betsy,
  Run up the bower so high
And see if your father
  Is a-riding near by."

"O father, dear father,
  Ride home with great haste;
There is trouble at the castle,
  There's trouble, indeed.

"There's blood in the kitchen
  And there's blood in the hall,
And here lies your lady
  Dead close by the wall."

False Lamkin was hung
  On a gallows so high,
And the false maid was burned
  In a furnace close by.

G

On July 7, 1933, Mrs. Ellen M. Sullivan of Springfield, Vermont, sang to Phillips Barry and Mrs. Flanders what she had called "Tumkin."

H. H. F., *Collector*
July 7, 1933

Tumkin

"Keep your doors well bolted
And your windows well pinned up
For fear William Tom King would come up."

He stole her jewels
And he stole her rings

And he stole her watches
And many precious things.

There was blood in the kitchen
And blood in the hall;
There was blood in the library
And blood on (in) the wall.

[*Old notes by H. H. F. found with this text state that Mrs.
Sullivan said of Tom King (Lamkin): "Tom King was com-
panion to Dick Turpin. They went to England. They never
killed anyone." Then followed*:]

There's blood in the kitchen
And blood in the hall;
There's blood in the parlor
And blood on the wall.

[*Then Mrs. Sullivan added, "Will Turpin had a noted
horse. He used to be arrested for stealing. He painted the
fetlocks of the horse. When he was haled into court, Turpin
hid 'Black Bess' in an alleyway of a hotel and fed him
through a window."*]

H

*The following is a copy of lines written down by Louise
Rogers Clough (Mrs. O. F.) of Poultney, Vermont, and
mailed to H. H. F. They represent stanzas of a ballad recalled by Mrs. Clough and her mother, Harriet Jane Burdick
Rogers (100 years old), originally learned from Mrs. Rogers'
grandmother, Cynthia Morgan, who was born in Poultney,
Vermont. Both Mrs. Clough and her mother were born in
Milford, New Hampshire. Mrs. Clough very much wanted
to know the story involved in these verses.*

H. H. F., Collector
November 12, 1957

Beau Lamkin

One day as the lord was gone from his home,
Who should be so bold as Beau Lamkin to come;
He knock-ed and knock-ed, and knock-ed again.
Who was so ready as the false nurse to let him in.

.   .   .   .

They pricked that little baby and pricked him again,
They pricked that little baby with a silver bodkin.
"He will not be soothed by breast milk or pap,
So come down, my fair lady, and hold him on your lap."

When the lord came home and opened the door,
He saw his son and lady lie dead on the floor.
Beau Lamkin he was hung on a gallows so high;
The false nurse she was burnt in a fire close by.

Index

(Figures in parentheses indicate the Child number)

317

Geographical Index

CONNECTICUT

Cheshire:	Mrs. G. C. Erskine, 67 C, 74 G
Litchfield:	Charles Webb, 84 U
West Cornwall:	Oscar Degreenia, 84 E

MAINE

Bridgewater:	Charles Finnemore, 81 I
Ellsworth Falls:	Mrs. Annie Tate Moore, 75 I
Hampden:	Mrs. Susan M. Harding, 93 B
Kingman:	Mrs. Margaret McPhail Morris, 93 A
Littleton:	Arthur Walker, 53 C, 81 D
Mars Hill:	Steven Barlow, 84 F
Monticello:	Miss Annie Syphers, 81 E
Searsport:	Mrs. Bertha J. Kneeland, 75 E
Sherman Mills:	Albert Cox, 84 M
Springfield:	Mrs. Hattie E. Smith, 84 N
Stacyville:	Eldin Colsie, 81 B
	Hanford Hayes, 73 E, 81 H
Vanceboro:	Mrs. Roy Blanchard, 81 C
York:	Mrs. Lilla Bracey, 73 G
	Alonzo Lewis, 53 D

MASSACHUSETTS

Concord:	Mrs. Anna Rainsford French Bush, 84 T
New Bedford:	Mrs. Sarah Taylor, 75 A
North Attleboro:	Mrs. Mabel White Lansing, 76 B
Savoy:	Miss Winifred Haskins, 74 C

NEW HAMPSHIRE

Charlestown:	Orlon Merrill, 53 M, 81 F, 84 R
Colebrook:	Mrs. Belle Richards, 53 E, 75 H, 84 D
Columbia:	George A. Jackson, 67 A
East Jaffrey:	Mrs. Lena Bourne Fish, 53 T, 75 C, 79 B, 84 K[1, 2]
Hanover:	Mrs. Frederic P. Lord, 75 D